Heal yourself with Crystals

Heal yourself with Crystals

Crystal medicine for body, emotions and spirit

HAZEL RAVEN

A GODSFIELD BOOK
www.godsfieldpress.com

First published in Great Britain in 2005
by Godsfield Press,
a division of Octopus Publishing Group Ltd
2–4 Heron Quays, London E14 4JP

Copyright © Octopus Publishing Group Ltd 2005
Text copyright © Hazel Raven 2005

ISBN 1 84181 263 3
EAN 9781841812632

A CIP catalogue record for this book is available
from the British Library

Printed and bound in China

10 9 8 7 6 5 4 3 2 1

DISCLAIMER
This book is not intended as an alternative to
personal medical advice. The reader should consult
a physician in all matters relating to health and
particularly in respect of any symptoms which may
require diagnosis or medical attention.

Contents

Introduction

Crystals have been used for thousands of years for decoration, physical adornment, healing, protection, magic and in religious ceremonies. They are the most organized and stable examples of physical matter in the natural world and as such they represent the lowest state of entropy (disorder) possible.

All crystalline structures are formed of mathematically precise and orderly three-dimensional arrangements of atoms. This is the crystal lattice, which confers a high level of stability. It also gives crystals their unique colours, hardness and physical, geometrical and energetic properties. Gemstones and crystals have an amazing capacity to absorb, reflect and radiate light in the form of intelligent fields of stable energy that

Wearing crystals

- Gems have traditionally been worn on the fingers to symbolize authority, spirituality or union, or to carry specific beneficial energies to certain parts of the body.

- Ancient rulers wore crowns set with precious gemstones to prove their importance.

- Worn around the wrist and arm, crystals influence and affect the side of the body on which you wear them.

- Wearing crystals around the neck in a visible position allows the sun's rays to pass through the stones, thereby stimulating them to release their beneficial energy into the physical and subtle bodies.

- The tradition of ear piercing dates back to antiquity, when earrings were worn to protect the ears from ghosts. Ear ornaments were part of the large number of amulets used to protect the openings of the body from dangerous malevolent spirits. Earrings also serve to balance the right and left hemispheres of the brain and will work on acupressure points of the ear itself.

- Rubies were worn in the navel of belly dancers to excite passion. This custom is being revived with the current interest in body piercing.

Jade   Amber   Ruby

increase the flow of vital life-force within the human physical and subtle anatomy. By applying this stable energy or crystal resonance in a coherent, focused way to dysfunctional energy systems, they holistically restore stability and balance. This results in the releasing of dis-ease, bringing about restructuring and alignment.

Ancient wisdom

Humans have always searched for ways to beautify themselves. Carrying crystals as protective amulets or wearing them as jewellery are the simplest ways to utilize their natural potential. Evidence has been found for the use of gemstones as jewellery as long ago as the Palaeolithic Age.

Perhaps the first written accounts of crystal healing came from the ancient Egyptians who gave detailed recipes for using gemstones such as Malachite for healing and protection. The ancient Egyptians also used Lapis Lazuli, Carnelian and Libyan Desert Glass (Golden Tektite). The Incas used Emerald, the Aztecs Obsidian, the Chinese Jade, and the Tibetans and Native Americans both used Turquoise. Smoky Quartz, Malachite, Amber, Shale and Jet were all used for adornment by the Celts.

We still have available the written knowledge of the Ayurvedic and Tantric scholars of the Indian subcontinent who knew the amazing potential of precious stones. In Vedic astrology (the *Vedas* are the primary source of Hindu philosophy) gemstones such

What is disease?

- **Conventional medicine** recognizes illness as a pattern of tests and symptoms that lead to the diagnosis of a named disease. It is normally assumed that diseases will have identifiable causes, for example infections, injuries and chemical imbalances in the body.

- **Oriental medicine** believes disease is brought about by different means: internal causes (the emotions); external causes (the weather); and various other causes such as bacteria, viruses, drugs, pollutants and diet.

- **Modern complementary medicine** sees dis-ease as a state that results from physical, emotional, mental or spiritual imbalances, which cause you to be ill at ease with some aspect of yourself. Cause could therefore include such things as negative thinking, suppressed emotions, an addictive personality or other behaviour traits.

as Rubies, Emeralds, Diamonds, Blue and Yellow Sapphires are reported to work through physicochemical and electrochemical means. They are 'prescribed' and are either worn as jewellery or taken orally as pastes or oxides to influence the biomagnetic sheath (the aura), as well as working through the nervous, lymphatic and *nadis* (see page 19) systems.

Emerald   Blue Sapphire   Yellow Sapphire   Turquoise

How crystals are formed

The majority of crystals used for crystal healing are minerals, solid substances created during the cooling, formative stages of the Earth's development some 5 billion years ago. The rocks where these crystals are found are aggregates (mixtures) of minerals and are described as igneous, sedimentary or metamorphic, depending on how they were formed.

For a mineral to qualify as a crystal, the atoms that make it up must normally be arranged in a systematic, regular, orderly and repeating three-dimensional structure. These arrangements determine the crystal's properties, including its hardness, colour and type of symmetry (a crystal is always symmetrical along at least one axis).

Today X-rays are used to analyze crystal structures. In the past, analysis was based on observation of the crystal's shape, a difficult and sometimes confusing process. Crystals of the same substance, for example Quartz, can seem almost infinitely variable in the sizes and shapes in which they are found. Adding to this confusion, most minerals occur as aggregates or crystals that rarely show perfect crystal shapes.

The characteristic shape of a crystal is known as its habit. In gem minerals it has been noticed that a different habit can occur in crystals of the same mineral that come from different localities or are of a different colour. For example, the blue-green form of Beryl (Aquamarine) is usually found as long prismatic crystals, while the pink form (Morganite) forms short tabular crystals.

When a mineral has a chemical composition the same as another mineral, but crystallizes in a different arrangement, the effect is termed polymorphism. Diamond and Graphite are perhaps the best-known example of this. Both are crystalline forms of the element Carbon.

Other types of 'crystals'

Crystal healing uses other natural substances as crystals, even though they do not have the regular atomic structure and properties that define crystals for geologists.

- **Amorphous crystals** Some crystals were formed so rapidly (usually in igneous rocks as they cooled) that no crystal structure had a chance to form. These are described as amorphous ('without definite form'). Obsidian is an example.

- **Extraterrestrial origins** Tektites are amorphous objects that may have been formed by meteor impact some 15 million years ago, or which may themselves be a type of meteorite. Moldavite is an example.

- **Pseudomorphs ('false forms')** These are minerals formed by an alteration to another substance that still manages to retain its original external shape. Wood Opal is an example, formed when Silica replaces the woody tissue of trees.

- **Organic origins** Amber is fossilized tree resin, Pearl is produced by oysters and other shellfish, and Coral is the skeletons of the tiny sea creatures that live together to form coral reefs and islands.

- **Metals** Pure metals, such as copper nuggets, may also be used as crystals.

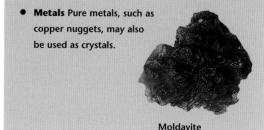

Moldavite

The physical properties of crystals

Crystals can be identified and classified in a number of ways, but their colour, hardness and type are perhaps the most important from a crystal healing perspective.

Colour

Crystals provide a strong, stable, focused, durable colour and are more powerful than just using colour therapy alone. Each major visible colour has a particular quality linked to the chakra with which it resonates. An understanding of the nature of the chakras (see page 18) and their energetic links to the body's physiology is all that is needed to select a particular coloured crystal for spiritual development or to ameliorate a specific dis-ease or emotional state. For simple colour healing with crystals just choose the colour you intuitively feel drawn towards.

There is no single cause of colour in crystals. Some of the visible colour comes from the chemical composition. The arrangement in space of the atoms in the crystal's structure also affects the colour, because they affect light rays passing through. These light rays are reflected and refracted (bent) by the crystal structure and so, depending on the way the light is distorted, display a particular colour.

Hardness

Hardness describes how easily a crystal can be scratched. In 1812 a German mineralogist, Friedrich Mohs, chose ten well-known and easily obtainable minerals and arranged them in order of their 'scratch hardness' to serve as standards of comparison. The Mohs scale still forms the universally accepted standard.

The numbers on the Mohs scale have no quantitative meaning, they represent an order only. Minerals that are categorized with a high number on the Mohs scale will scratch those rated at a lower number. The Mohs scale starts at hardness 1 for Talc, and ends at hardness 10, which is Diamond. When comparing crystals, it is useful to know that a fingernail falls between 2 and 3 on the scale, a knife blade and a piece of window glass both register between 5 and 6, and a steel file between 6 and 7.

Hardness 7 on the Mohs scale (represented by Quartz) is important, as any crystal must be at least this hard if it is to be worn regularly as jewellery. Crystals with a hardness less than 5 cleanse emotional imbalances by absorbing them. Amber, Apophyllite, Fluorite, Malachite, Selenite, Jet, Coral, Celestite, Chrysocolla and Calcite can all be used to soak up emotional debris.

Aquamarine

Diamond

Types of crystal

Natural

A natural crystal is just that, one that is in its natural growth formation, that has not been fashioned in any way. Natural crystals come in many forms and a nugget (lump of pure metal) is as natural as a blade (Kyanite forms in these fan-like clusters of thin crystals). Massive crystals have no crystalline structure visible to the naked eye, although it can be seen under a microscope.

Natural Blue Kyanite blade

may be large or small (some may be too small to see). Crystal with terminations have a natural or fashioned (artificially shaped) point at

Amethyst with single termination

one or both ends. Single terminated crystals, with a point at one end only, are used to direct the flow of energy. The other end can be left raw or be fashioned into a flat end. The pointed end is positive (male), the other end is negative (female).

Raw

A raw crystal is a piece that has been taken from a larger natural crystal and that has not been shaped or polished. They can sometimes be quite sharp and jagged.

Raw Yellow Fluorite

Tumbled

Tumbled stones are pieces of crystal that have been polished with successively fine grades of abrasive gravel until they are smooth, shiny and durable. Only crystals with a hardness of 7 or over should be worn as jewellery regularly.

Tumbled Moonstone

Terminations

When minerals are free to develop without restriction they are bound by naturally occurring crystal faces, and these are called terminations or points. Natural terminations

Wands

Facet wands focus and direct healing energy. They can be manufactured from any natural gemstone or quartz material. Fashioned wands are long and slender and have six straight sides with a small point at each end of the wand.

Rose Quartz wand

Fashioned

Fashioned (artificially shaped) crystals include wands, standing points, pyramids, spheres and eggs. They can be created from any crystals that are hard enough to be cut to shape and then polished to a high shine.

Onyx sphere

Selecting crystals

Choosing which crystal to use may seem a daunting task, as there are so many to choose from. However, as all crystals are attuned to a particular resonance and have particular properties, it is possible to look them up in a book and find out which is the most appropriate to use in particular circumstances.

Alternatively, see which crystal attracts you. By following your instincts and trusting your intuition you begin to trust yourself. You can confirm your intuitive or natural selection by dowsing with a pendulum, kinesiology (muscle strength reaction) or by passing your hand over the crystal to see if you can feel an energetic connection.

If you make a strong energetic connection, you may feel an 'electric' charge or tingling on your skin or in your hands, pulsing or twitching in your fingers or hand, sensations of heat or cold, a flush or wave of heat through your body or feelings of being enclosed by the crystal energy field.

If you are still unsure which crystal to choose, then opt for Clear Quartz, the 'master healer' (see page 12).

Looking after your crystals

- Once you have chosen your crystals, look after them properly. Allowing others to touch your personal crystals or jewellery will result in them becoming contaminated with foreign emanations that may not be compatible with your energy field.

- Store crystals carefully, because if stones of differing hardness are kept together (for example in a pouch) then the harder ones will scratch and damage the softer ones, even when they are all tumbled stones. Remember that some crystals such as Celestite or Kunzite can lose their colour in strong sunlight.

- Crystals worn as jewellery must be of at least hardness 7 on Mohs scale (see page 9). Never wear a porous crystal in the shower or bath or when swimming. Take pendants and similar jewellery off at night and place them on your bedside table. Check chains and other fastenings regularly to prevent breakages, and store any jewellery you are not actually wearing in its original packaging.

Clear Quartz

Clear Quartz is known as the 'master healer' or 'cure all' because it contains the full spectrum of the visible white light – a broad spectrum healing energy which clears dis-ease from all levels. Clear Quartz crystals stabilize, focus and amplify vital life-force, which heightens natural healing power and healing potential as well as stimulating personal growth and spiritual development.

The resonance of Clear Quartz crystals will swiftly go to the area in need of restructuring. This energy is self-regulating, resulting in optimum release of negative patterns or miasms (see page 138) that may have lodged in any level of the subtle body.

Clear Quartz crystals can resonate with the liquid crystals in the physical body, cellular elements that include cell salts, lymphatic vessels, fatty tissue, red and white blood cells and the pineal gland.

On a subtle-energetic level Clear Quartz creates carrier waves of pure vibrant energy that improve health and rejuvenate body functions by stimulating the energy flow of the meridians and chakras, so cleansing the aura of stagnant energy.

Clear Quartz is used to focus, amplify and direct spiritual energy, and to channel life-force, so releasing stress and stopping burn-out and energy depletion. A Clear Quartz crystal with a single termination or a facet wand is normally used for this technique but other members of the Quartz family (such as Amethyst, Rutile Quartz, Smoky Quartz, Citrine or Rose Quartz) are also suitable.

When used in meditation Clear Quartz stimulates harmonious focused brain activity, which aids peace and relaxation.

Programming Clear Quartz

Normally only Clear Quartz crystals are modifiable or 'programmable', as other crystals automatically contain their own specific resonance or natural signature.

YOU WILL NEED

1 Clear Quartz crystal

WHAT TO DO

1 To program your Clear Quartz crystal, simply hold it to your third eye chakra (between and just above your physical eyes) and concentrate on the purpose for which you wish to use it. Remain positive while you allow your crystal to fill with this energy.

2 You could also state the intention of the programming out loud, for example 'I program this crystal for healing' or for love, abundance, meditation, dream interpretation or other purpose of your choice.

Clear Quartz

Cleansing crystals

It is important to purify your crystals before and after use. This ensures that any residual disharmonies are removed and your crystals are filled with positive energy. Choose a safe cleansing process. Some crystals are soft and water-soluble, other delicate crystal groups – such as Celestite or Selenite – will separate in water. Salt water can damage or split crystalline structures, making the stone appear dull or cloudy or change colour. The damage will be irreparable. Salt will extract water from Opals quickly.

Cleansing techniques

- **Water** For those crystals that can be cleansed with water, use a stream, waterfall, river or spring water. As the water flows over your crystal hold the intention that all negativity will be washed away and the crystal re-energized.

- **Salt** Although contradictory, because salt can damage crystals, cleansing with sea salt is an accepted method and is widely accepted as necessary to remove stagnant negative energy that cannot be removed by any other method. Be aware of the problems. Suitable crystals can be placed in a large bowl of sea salt (brush all the salt off the crystal afterwards). Opals and other susceptible crystals can be placed in a small glass dish that is embedded in a larger dish of salt.

- **Smudging** This is an excellent ancient form of purification for your crystals, for you and for your healing or meditation space. Allow the smoke to pass around the crystal to remove residual disharmonies. If you are indoors keep a window open to let the stagnant energy out.

- **Sound** Using sound to cleanse your crystals is very effective, especially for purifying several at the same time. Use a crystal singing bowl and a bell, tingshas (small Tibetan cymbals) or tuning fork.

- **Specialist cleansing products** These crystal, angelic and aromatherapy cleansers come in atomizer bottles and clean all crystals and the environment instantly.

Smudge stick

Tingshas

Gem essences

Gem essences allow the subtle vibrations of crystals to interact with our subtle-energy fields to provide crystal healing. They work in harmony with the body and are self-adjusting and natural, containing nothing more than subtly energized water. They can be used by anyone of any age, combined with any conventional or complementary medicines and treatments, and will even benefit pets, flowers, trees and plants.

How to prepare a gem essence

When activated by solar energy (natural sunlight), crystals readily transfer their vibratory signature into water. Impurity-free distilled water has no energetic signature, making it the ideal medium, but you can also use spring or mineral water.

YOU WILL NEED

Crystal(s) of your choice, natural or tumbled
Distilled water
Clear glass or quartz crystal bowl
Alcohol (brandy is suitable)
Large amber bottle to store the mother essence
Amber glass dropper bottle as a dosage bottle

NOTE: Amber glass protects the gem essence from exposure to light.

WHAT TO DO

1 Cleanse your crystals and sterilize the other equipment. Place the crystals in a bowl of distilled water.

2 Place the bowl in full direct early morning sunlight on a cloudless day. Leave for 2–3 hours to imprint the subtle-energy of the crystals into the water. Always take the bowl in before noon, when the sun's energy changes and becomes draining.

3 Measure the volume of essence you have made. Pour it into the mother bottle and add twice its volume of alcohol.

4 Transfer seven drops from the mother bottle into the dropper bottle. Fill with a mixture of

one-third alcohol, two-thirds distilled water. Use all water if you prefer, in which case keep the dropper bottle refrigerated and use the contents within seven days.

5 Label the bottles with the name of the crystal(s), date made and the number and frequency of drops required.

The container method

You should use this method if you are making an essence from a crystal that should not be placed in water or is toxic.

YOU WILL NEED

Crystal(s) of your choice, natural or tumbled
Small glass
Clear glass or quartz crystal bowl
Distilled water
Alcohol (brandy is suitable)
Large amber bottle to store the mother essence
Amber glass dropper bottle as a dosage bottle

1 Place the crystal(s) in a separate small glass within your glass bowl of water. The water will not touch the crystal(s), but the subtle-energy vibrations can still pass through.

2 Follow steps 2–5 of 'How to Prepare a Gem Essence' (see opposite).

Using gem essences

- Normally seven drops are taken three times a day, but essences can be also taken as often as required. Place the drops directly from the dosage bottle under your tongue, or dissolve them in mineral water and sip it slowly.

- Drops can be placed directly onto the meridian or pulse points, or added to bath water or massage oil. They can be dissolved in distilled water in an atomizer bottle and sprayed around the body.

The subtle body

The subtle anatomy is composed of the aura, meridians and chakras. These subtle-energy systems are invisible to most people, although the talent to see them can be developed. They are contained in and surround the physical body. While not anatomically recognized by conventional medical science, they are nevertheless metaphysically connected with all the different systems within the physical body.

Aura

Meridian system

Aura

The peoples of ancient cultures knew and understood that beyond its physical form the human body is a pulsing, dynamic field of energy. Through observation they developed an understanding of these basic fundamental subtle-energies that surround and permeate the human form. In Sanskrit this subtle-energy field is called *kosas* (body sheaths), while in modern complementary medicine it is known as the biomagnetic energy field or aura.

The word aura comes from the Greek word *avra*, meaning breeze. It looks like a luminous egg of pulsing, moving, dynamic energy that surrounds and interpenetrates the physical body. The aura consists of seven levels that correlate to the seven master chakras. These levels begins with the seen (the physical body) and progress to more subtle and refined vibrations as we go further away from the physical.

All auras are different and change constantly as our thoughts, moods, environment and state of health change. A person with a spiritual aura is an inspirational joy to be with. As people develop spiritually they do have an amazing glow around their crown chakra.

Auric damage and depletion is caused by ill health, negative thought patterns, environmental pollutants, bad dietary habits, addictive substances, stress or poor breathing techniques. It can be repaired with the correct use and placement of crystals and gemstones.

Meridians

In Chinese and Ayurvedic medicine, health is seen as the fluent and harmonious movement of energies at subtle levels. This energy has various names. The Indian yogis call it *prana*, as do Ayurveda practitioners (Ayurveda is the traditional holistic healing system of the Indian subcontinent). To Tibetan lamas it is *lung-gom*, while it is known as *sakia-tundra* or to the followers of Shinto (the indigenous religion of Japan). The Chinese call it *chi* or *qi*. Loosely translated, all these terms mean 'life energy' or 'life-force'.

Life energy is considered to have clearly distinct and established pathways, definite direction of flow, and characteristic behaviour as well defined as any other circulatory system in the physical body, such as blood and the vascular system. In Chinese traditional medicine, these pathways are the meridians through which *chi* flows.

The meridian theory arose from thousands of years of medical practice in China. The word meridian came into the English language through a French translation of the Chinese term *jing-luo*. *Jing* means 'to go through' or 'a thread in a fabric'; *luo* means 'something that connects or attaches' or 'a net'.

The Chinese, in acupuncture, developed the use of needles to unblock these pathways. In shiatsu, the Japanese use direct thumb and finger pressure on acupuncture meridian points to achieve similar results. Through increased awareness of meridians one can practise crystal therapy more effectively, as meridians provide profound insight into the disease pathway and are therefore a most useful diagnostic therapy tool.

Chakras

Chakras are funnel-shaped spinning energy vortexes of multicoloured light. The word chakra comes from the Sanskrit and means 'wheel' or 'disc'. Chakras are vitally important for your physical health, emotional wellbeing and spiritual growth. Each master chakra is a linkage point associated with specific organs and endocrine glands. They must always be seen as a complete integrated system that works holistically.

Chakras can also be viewed as step-down transformers for higher-frequency subtle-energies. They process this subtle-energy and convert it into chemical, hormonal and cellular changes in the body. Each chakra vibrates at a different vibrational frequency and on a different note.

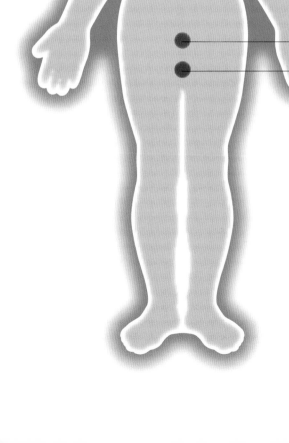

Crown chakra

Third eye chakra

Throat chakra

Heart chakra

Solar plexus chakra

Sacral chakra

Root chakra

The major chakras

- The **root chakra** is located at the base of the spine. Its Sanskrit name is *muladhara*, and its symbol is a four-petal crimson lotus flower around a yellow square containing a downward-pointing white triangle.

- The **sacral chakra** is located in the sexual organs. Its Sanskrit name is *svadhisthana*, and its symbol is a six-petal orange lotus flower containing a second lotus flower and an upward-pointing crescent moon in a white circle.

- The **solar plexus chakra** is located at the diaphragm. Its Sanskrit name is *manipura*, and its symbol is a ten-petal yellow lotus flower whose centre contains a red downward-pointing triangle.

- The **heart chakra** is located in the region of the physical heart. Its Sanskrit name is *anahata*, and its symbol is a 12-petal green lotus flower whose centre contains a green circle and two intersecting triangles making up a six-pointed star representing balance.

- The **throat chakra** is located at the base of the throat. Its Sanskrit name is *vishuddha*, and its symbol is a 16-petal blue lotus flower whose centre contains a downwards-pointing triangle within which is a circle representing the full moon.

- The **third eye chakra** is located between and just above the physical eyes. Its Sanskrit name is *ajna*, and its symbol is two large white lotus petals on each side of a white circle, within which is a downwards-pointing triangle.

- The **crown chakra** is located at the crown of the head. Its Sanskrit name is *sahasrara*, and its symbol is the thousand-petal white lotus flower.

Energy channels

To yogis and practitioners of Ayurveda, (life-force or subtle-energy) is the equivalent of *chi* in traditional Chinese medicine. *Prana* flows through the human body through the *nadis* (channels). There are thousands of *nadis* but the three main ones are *sushumna*, *pingala* and *ida*.

Sushumna, the central channel, is situated inside the spinal column. *Pingala* and *ida* start respectively from the right and left nostrils, move up past the temporal lobes to the crown of the head and course downwards to the base of the spine. These two major *nadis* intersect with each other and also with the *sushumna*. The seven master chakras lie along the *sushumna* at its junctions with the other two channels.

There are literally hundreds of smaller chakras and they are all interrelated in a very complex system throughout the human body. In addition, other non-physical chakras lie outside the physical body. The best-known of these are the earth star chakra, located beneath the feet, and the soul star chakra, located above the head.

The major chakras, the moderators of subtle-energy, are envisioned in the *Vedas* (the primary source of Hindu philosophy) as sacred lotus flowers. Each chakra has a lotus with a different number of petals. These relate to Sanskrit symbolism concerning the configuration of subtle nerves, the *nadis* (think of these as the roots of the lotus flowers) that emanate from the particular region of the spinal column where the chakra is located, and also to the meaning of the particular vowels and consonants that make up the chakra's Sanskrit name.

The endocrine system

The endocrine system is responsible for the production of hormones which, in turn, are responsible for our emotional states and our energy levels. Hormones are the body's chemical messengers that course through the bloodstream to stimulate or inhibit the activity of their target cells, tissues and organs. They regulate the body's processes — everything from digestion, metabolism and reproduction to emotions, general health and wellbeing. Any change in the level of a particular hormone affects not only the body process it controls but also the entire system.

Hormones can be thought of as the life-giving force that animates you physically, mentally and emotionally. While orthodox medicine describes our physical system in terms of chemistry, complementary medicine now understands that for any chemical action to happen a change in the electromagnetic energy of the body must occur first. This energy emanates from the mind and explains the mind-body link to our physical, emotional, mental and spiritual health.

Subtle energy is non-physical, dynamic and ever-changing. Because it is non-physical it is not bound by the laws of matter. It is linked to the endocrine system as an expression of consciousness or spiritual evolution and relativity perception.

The major endocrine glands

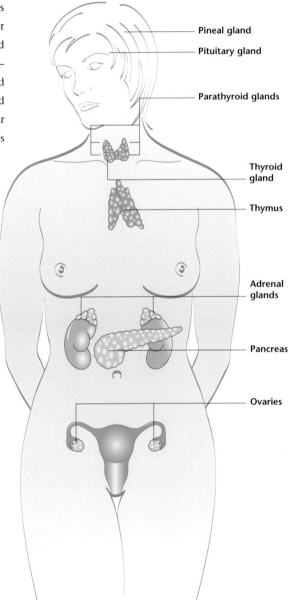

- Pineal gland
- Pituitary gland
- Parathyroid glands
- Thyroid gland
- Thymus
- Adrenal glands
- Pancreas
- Ovaries

THE PITUITARY GLAND

The pituitary gland is the master gland that controls the action of other glands in the endocrine system. It also produces hormones that control growth and sexual development. Its subtle-energy functions are those of the higher brain — knowledge, understanding and discernment. Malfunctions may lead to confusion, depression, obsessional thinking, chronic exhaustion and sensitivity to pollutants.

THE PINEAL GLAND

The pineal gland produces the hormone melatonin, which controls our body rhythms, our sleeping and our waking. Its subtle-energy functions are intuition, insight, inspiration and imagination, seeing auras, sensing the desires of other people or hearing their thoughts. Malfunctions may lead to headaches, nightmares, hallucinations and learning difficulties.

THYROID AND PARATHYROID GLANDS

These glands are situated close to each other. The thyroid produces hormones that regulate many aspects of our metabolism, including our energy levels. The parathyroid glands are responsible for calcium levels in the blood, an important role as even a small decrease can have a harmful effect on nerves and muscles. Together their subtle-energy functions are communication, creativity and self expression. Malfunctions may lead to perfectionism, the inability to express emotions and blocked creativity.

THE THYMUS

The thymus also forms part of the immune system. It helps to produce the white blood cells that protect us from infections. Its subtle-energy functions are our beliefs about love, interconnectedness, relationships and developing compassion. Malfunctions of this subtle-energy may lead to fear of betrayal, co-dependency and melancholia.

THE ADRENAL GLANDS

The adrenal glands are responsible for the 'fight or flight' response, the adrenaline (epinephrine) rush we get when we are excited or stressed. They also produce corticosteroid hormones that regulate blood volume and pressure, metabolism, and inflammatory reactions in the body. Their subtle-energy functions are grounded reality, stability, self-preservation and survival. Malfunctions may lead to mental lethargy, 'spaciness', anxiety and being incapable of finding inner stillness.

THE PANCREAS

The pancreas produces insulin, the hormone that regulates blood sugar levels. Imbalance in blood sugar levels leads to diabetes. Its subtle-energy functions are personal power, igniting the imagination, manifesting dreams and ambitions and intellectual activity. Malfunctions may lead to addictive personality traits, anger, rage and oversensitivity to criticism. A person with such a malfunction may need to be in control, have low self-esteem, be overly concerned with status and power and may manipulate others for gain.

OVARIES AND TESTES

The ovaries (in women) and the testes (in men) are endocrine glands as well as being part of the reproductive system. The ovaries produce the female sex hormones oestrogen and progesterone, and the testes produce the male sex hormone testosterone. The subtle-energy functions of both these glands are vitality, attraction, magnetism, emotional stability, desire, social awareness and partnerships. Malfunctions may lead to emotional instability, feelings of isolation, personality disorders related to the emotions, and being besieged by constant sexual fantasies and desires for new sexual experiences and partners.

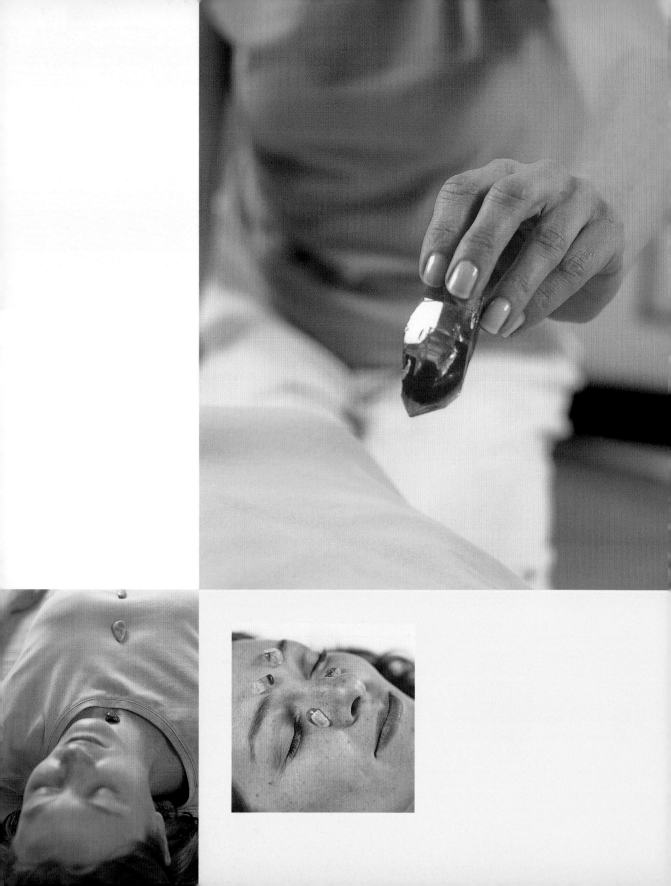

PART 1

CRYSTALS TO
HEAL YOUR BODY

Crystals and your body

Crystal healing, like other complementary therapies, focuses on the underlying causes of physical ailments, the dis-ease behind the disease. Dis-ease is the state that results from physical, emotional, mental or spiritual imbalances that cause you to be ill at ease with some aspect of yourself. This state may then make itself known by affecting your health. When the physical body develops any form of illness it is often trying to bring something to our attention.

The Chinese were probably the first to chronicle the link between physical ill health and dis-ease several thousand years ago, but the body-mind connection has been understood by almost every civilization throughout history.

This holistic approach is a vital component in the search for wellness, especially if the same ailment keeps recurring or the same area of the body keeps being affected.

Crystals and gemstones work holistically through resonance, using subtle-energies. By applying this subtle-energy resonance in a coherent, focused way to dysfunctional energy systems, they restore stability and balance. Crystal healing thus allows you to reconnect with your natural harmony by stimulating your body's inherent healing mechanisms and increasing the flow of life-force. This results in the releasing of dis-ease, bringing restructuring and alignment. Obviously there can be physical causes for illness, but not everyone exposed to a particular virus or bacterium develops the illness.

Healing is a uniquely personal process. If we listen to our bodies and learn to understand their language and their messages, we become increasingly aware of the connections between body, mind and spirit. Crystal therapy works to harmonize all parts of our psyches so that we become seamless, integrated, radiant whole beings.

You may be ignoring your body's messages, not because you intend or want to, but because you are simply unaware of them amid the pressures of modern-day living. Most people react to illness by trying to eliminate the symptoms as quickly as possible with direct conventional medical intervention.

There is nothing wrong in seeking relief from unpleasant or distressing symptoms but, if you want your body to truly be dis-ease free, you will also need to understand why you are ill. Remember, we are complex beings, not just our manifesting symptoms or medical label. The body is not simply a machine or collection of chemicals.

A healthy environment

A holistic approach to health considers our surroundings as well as our personal physical, emotional and spiritual states. The atmosphere of our homes and workplaces plays a vital role in our being healthy and feeling nurtured. The conditions in which we live and work have a lasting effect on our physical bodies. Using crystal healing to improve our environment or to counteract its effects on us can be an effective tool for promoting wellness and wellbeing.

POLLUTION

We are all subject to environmental pollutants and toxins, many of us are also affected by bad diets and the stress of city living. Taking a gem essence daily made from a detoxifying crystal such as Selenite or Herkimer Diamond can be very beneficial (see page 15 for information on making gem essences).

ELECTROMAGNETIC FIELDS

Over time, the effects of electromagnetic fields (EMFs) caused by anything powered by electricity can influence our biomagnetic sheath (the natural magnetic energy of the body, the aura), which in turn has a direct influence on the physical body. Many illnesses have been attributed to extended exposure to what has been termed electromagnetic smog. Black Tourmaline is extremely effective as a protective, grounding stone as it quickly deflects negative energy back to earth.

GEOPATHIC STRESS

Geopathic stress (GS) moves in thin focused lines. It is believed to be caused by underground streams, faults in the substrata of the Earth, large mineral deposits or negative ley lines. Sometimes only one person in the home shows signs of GS-related illness such as migraines, tiredness, depression, nightmares, aches and pains. Because GS flow lines are narrow, sometimes something as simple as just moving your bed can relieve the symptoms. Dowsing with a crystal pendulum over a plan of the building will help you discover where the GS lines fall.

Feng shui

- Feng shui is the ancient Oriental art of arranging our surroundings that promotes the modern idea of ecology and conservation. We all know tampering with nature disrupts the harmonious flow of the weather and damages the environment. By dwelling in oneness with the elemental forces and focussing on the subtle flow of *chi* (life-force) within our homes, we bring harmony to our lives.

- There are nine feng shui 'cures', all designed to repel, dispel or dissipate stagnant or harmful *chi*, and of these crystals are probably the most popular. Any negative *chi* that encounters a crystal is transformed.

- Large Amethyst geodes or Quartz clusters are very effective as room cleansers. Quartz obelisks are especially potent energy enhancers that magnetize or pull positive *chi* towards them.

Amethyst geode

Headaches

Tension headaches, also known as muscle contraction headaches, are probably the most common. They are felt above the eyes and on the back of the head, usually start in the morning, and intensify as the day progresses. Common causes include stress, depression, anxiety, poor posture, eye strain, and sleeping or working in awkward positions.

Migraines cause intense, unrelenting pain, usually on only one side of the head but sometimes spreading to the entire head. They occur when the blood vessels supplying the brain narrow and then widen, but what causes this to happen is unknown. However, attacks are sometimes triggered by eating particular foods or taking particular medications such as the contraceptive pill. Just before the pain starts, some sufferers experience warning symptoms such as tingling sensations (pins and needles), nausea and vomiting, or seeing flashing lights. Migraines are four times more common in women and appear to run in families. Although they can occur at any age, they peak between the mid-twenties and middle age.

Cluster headaches are a type of migraine. They cause intense pain on one side of the head, affecting the eye, temple, cheek and jaw. Men over the age of 30 are the most likely sufferers from these uncommon headaches which may be triggered by alcohol.

Premenstrual headaches may be migraines or tension headaches, and typically occur just before the start of a period.

Most headaches occur independently of any other illness. However, they can also be symptoms of many other illnesses, varying from flu to more serious disorders of the nervous system such as stroke or meningitis. Consulting your doctor if you have persistent or very severe headaches is therefore a sensible precaution.

Headache relief web crystals

- Amethyst crystals reach deep into the body to clear the source of the headache. A transformational stone, amethyst purifies the physical and subtle bodies and amplifies healing and spiritual energies. When consciously directed it will break down and transform blocked or stuck energies that may be causing the pain. It also aids restful sleep, relieving tension and stress which are major causes of headaches.

- Lapis sedates the conscious mind and is therefore good for relaxation. It can offer relief from physical pain and help with self-expression.

- Smoky Quartz draws discordant energy towards itself and absorbs it.

Amethyst

Lapis

Smoky Quartz

Headache relief web

This technique channels the painful, scattered energy away from your head. The web can also be used by those who suffer from sensitivity to noise, eye disorders or hearing disorders.

YOU WILL NEED

5 Smoky Quartz, with single terminations
1 small Amethyst, with single termination
1 Lapis, tumbled

WHAT TO DO

1 Lie down comfortably on the floor, using a yoga mat or pad if you prefer.

2 Place the five Smoky Quartz crystals around your body: one on your throat (with the termination pointing downwards); one beneath each foot (terminations pointing away from your feet); and one in each hand with the terminations pointing away from you.

3 Place the Amethyst underneath your head at the base of your skull with the termination pointing downwards.

4 Place the Lapis on your forehead, just above and between your eyes.

5 Relax your body by focussing on your breathing. As you breathe out, focus on the word 'release'. As you breathe in, focus on the word 'peace'.

6 Allow 20 minutes for your body to integrate the energies. Be ready to remove the crystals sooner if your intuition tells that you have integrated the crystal energy more quickly.

7 Cleanse your crystals after use (see page 13).

Therapy tip

- Carrying Smoky Quartz keeps you grounded in stressful situations because it draws in and absorbs discordant energy. An excellent crystal for bringing stability back to the physical body, it can be used after all therapy sessions to ground and focus your energy and prevent the condition know as a healing crisis.

Sinus congestion

Sinuses are air-filled cavities in your facial bones, situated around your nose and eyes. They are lined with membranes that secrete mucus, and narrow channels join them to the space at the back of your nose. If you have ever suffered from inflamed sinuses, perhaps after a very bad cold, you will know exactly where they are, because they will have been painful and tender.

Sinusitis (inflammation of the sinuses) and sinus congestion often follow a cold or a flare of allergic rhinitis (hay fever). For many people sinusitis means only a few days intense discomfort, but for others it becomes a long-lasting problem. Acute and chronic sinusitis can both cause nasal congestion, thick postnasal drip, cough, headache and fever. The headache that accompanies sinus problems is felt in the eyes, forehead, cheeks and the top of the head. Postnasal drip happens when the extra mucus produced in the inflamed sinuses trickles from the back of the nose down into the top of the throat.

Sinus congestion is linked to unexpressed emotions, to a build-up of tears waiting to be shed. To release these solidified tears often requires us to review our emotional health and attitudes, and to let go of long-held and self-imposed restraints.

Releasing crystals

- Apache Tears are glassy pebble-like solid cores of unaltered glass, from the decomposed Black Obsidian of the American south-west. They dissolve emotional blockages and relieve pain. Black Obsidian purges negativity from the meridian system (see page 17) and wands of Obsidian may be used instead of needles in acupuncture.

- Clear Calcite brings clarity and brilliance as it cleanses stagnant energy and emotional stress. It is used as a cure-all, for detoxification and as a crystal antiseptic. It also makes an excellent gem essence, which is used for new beginnings.

- Fluorite purifies and restructures subtle-energy patterns. It also helps you cleanse negative thoughts, feelings and emotional rubbish that you have dwelt on for years. As such it will improve all negative, degraded, chronic conditions.

Purple Fluorite

Apache Tear

Clear Calcite

Releasing

Crying is a great safety valve, but unfortunately many people were and are taught as children that it is a sign of weakness. This technique will not necessarily bring on floods of tears, but it may give you some insight into the times you did not allow yourself to weep. It uses the polarities of black and white cleansing crystals to purify the meridians (see page 17) associated with sinus congestion. The Purple or Blue Fluorite then restructures the subtle-energy patterns.

YOU WILL NEED

4 Apache Tears, natural
4 Clear Calcite or Rainbow Calcite, natural
4 Purple Fluorite, natural or tumbled

NOTE: You can use Rainbow Calcite instead of Clear Calcite, and Blue Fluorite instead of Purple Fluorite.

WHAT TO DO

1 Lie down comfortably on the floor, using a yoga mat or pad if you prefer.

2 Place the Apache Tears on your face, one just below each eye at the inner edge of the eye socket, the others at the beginning point of each eyebrow next to the nose. Leave these crystals in place for 5 minutes.

3 Replace the Apache Tears with the Clear Calcite crystals. Leave these crystals in place for 5 minutes.

4 Replace the Clear Calcite crystals with the Purple Fluorite crystals. Leave these crystals in place for 5 minutes.

5 Cleanse your crystals after use (see page 13).

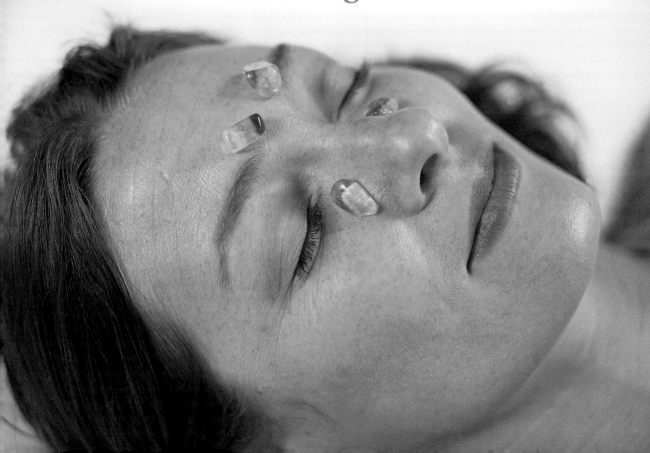

Colds and flu

As there are more than 200 respiratory viruses that can give someone a cold, it is not surprising that we catch them so often. The symptoms that go with a cold – runny nose, coughing, sneezing, nasal congestion, sore throat and fatigue – are not produced by the virus itself, but by your body's response to the infection. Colds usually clear up on their own in 7 to 10 days.

Flu (influenza) is also caused by respiratory viruses. The symptoms include chills, fever, headache, sore throat and muscle aches and pains. Getting plenty of rest is important when you have flu or a cold, and drinking plenty of fluids enables your body to stay hydrated which in turn helps clear mucus secretions.

As respiratory viruses mutate rapidly, new strains of colds and flu appear frequently, and so we remain susceptible to them. You can increase your resistance to colds and flu by eating a healthy diet, getting adequate rest and exercising moderately every day. Minimizing emotional stress is also a good preventative, as too much stress can weaken your immune system.

Gem essence

Taking this gem essence daily to support your immune system is an excellent way to minimize your susceptibility to catching colds and flu.

YOU WILL NEED

1 Aqua Aura Quartz, natural, with termination

WHAT TO DO

Make a gem essence (see page 14 for information on how to do this) and take it as directed.

Aqua Aura Quartz medicine

- Aqua Aura Quartz is produced when atoms of pure gold are bonded with Clear Quartz. This alchemical crystal strengthens the thymus gland, an important part of the immune system that helps to produce the white blood cells which defend our bodies from bacteria, viruses and similar attackers.

- These highly energized stones are an extremely powerful extension of the 'master healer' Clear Quartz (see page12), which contains a broad spectrum of healing energy that balances all body systems.

Aqua Aura Quartz

Breathing problems

All the cells in your body need a constant supply of oxygen to survive. Your respiratory system is responsible for providing this oxygen supply, so anything that affects your breathing can affect the rest of your body as well.

Breathing is automatic, and is controlled by the respiratory centre in the base of your brain, which prompts your diaphragm to contract about 12–20 times a minute when you are at rest. Your diaphragm is the powerful muscle just below your lungs that helps to create the changes in pressure that allow you to breathe in and out. You take air (oxygen) in and breathe carbon dioxide out.

Most of the respiratory system disorders that cause breathing problems are caused by infection with viruses or bacteria. Pneumonia varies in severity depending on whether it has been caused by viruses, bacteria or fungi, but it is an illness that always requires prompt medical treatment.

Infection is not the only cause of respiratory disorders. Asthma is caused by an allergic reaction and is often aggravated by air pollution. Exposure to harmful substances in the air, such as certain chemicals and dusts, is a risk in some types of work. The major cause of chronic long-term disorders such as emphysema and chronic bronchitis is, of course, smoking.

The lungs regulate respiration and are therefore responsible for the *chi* (life-force) of the entire body (see page 19). Grief impairs the energy of the lungs, for with grieving the body feels empty and hollow. Unresolved grief brings long-term feelings of loss, anguish, heartache, sadness and sorrow. Holding on to the past by grieving saps life-force; as even talking about negative experiences from the past can tear massive holes in the auric shell.

Gem essence

As Rutile Quartz has a perfect balance of cosmic light (the ancients thought it was captured sunlight), it sustains life and the vital life-force, and aids cellular regeneration. Use this gem essence to restore your vibrancy and vitality, and to ameliorate respiratory problems and chronic conditions.

YOU WILL NEED
1 Rutile Quartz, tumbled

WHAT TO DO
Make a gem essence (see page 14 for information on how to do this) and take it as directed.

Therapy tips

- You can use either clear or smoky Rutile Quartz. Both contain needles of titanium.

- Carrying or wearing Rutile Quartz aids vitality and optimism.

Rutile Quartz

Weakened immune system

The immune system is the body's defence mechanism. If you are prone to infections, you may have a weakened immune system. Increasing your life energy (*prana*), strengthens your immune system, which helps you fight off colds, flu and other ailments.

The immune system can also make mistakes. Autoimmune disorders are conditions in which the immune system attacks its own proteins, mistaking them for foreign invaders such as viruses and bacteria. Exactly what causes these disorders is not known, but they may have an emotional basis as well as environmental and physical causes.

The thymus gland, an important part of the immune system, is located between the heart and throat, where the collarbones meet. The thymus produces hormones that stimulate growth in early life. It also plays a purifying role in the body by stimulating the production of lymphocytes (a particular type of white blood cell). White blood cells attack invading organisms and provide immunity.

When the thymus gland is stressed because of infection or emotional distress, it needs an energy boost. Tapping on your thymus area several times, moving your taps in a clockwise direction, is an excellent way to awaken and balance your immune system, thereby increasing your life energy. You can perform this exercise every day.

The thymus can also be strengthened using crystal healing. Placing a Turquoise, Chrysocolla or Aquamarine crystal over your thymus increases your life energy and strengthens your body's natural defence system. These crystals can also help you express yourself, build self-confidence, stimulate your creativity and balance the energies of the heart.

Turquoise medicine

- Turquoise calms and soothes the emotions. It is an excellent meditation stone that can help you go with your own 'flow', find your perfect life-path with courage and fortitude and feel compassion for yourself. It shields your energy field (aura) from anger, hatred, envy and hostility.

- This crystal releases stress by relaxing the shoulders and upper body. When you are relaxed, you can breathe more deeply, taking in more oxygen, which flushes out toxins and balances your hormones.

- It protects you from the impressions and influences of others. It opens the gateway to understanding the archetypal realms, promotes physical, mental and emotional stability, and helps you recognize the dramas you may be caught up in. Use Turquoise to help you to step out of your situation and see the underlying emotions. Once you understand your personal 'drama', you can change it for one that is more in tune with the life you really want.

- Turquoise helps you accept and express who you are. Suppressing your individuality drains your life-force, which leaves you vulnerable to infections, autoimmune diseases and other negative influences.

Turquoise

Life-force web

You can use Turquoise and its related crystals to create a life-force web. This powerful healing technique strengthens your immune system and increases your ability to defend yourself against allergies, infections and unwanted influences.

YOU WILL NEED

8 Turquoise, tumbled

NOTE: You can use Chrysocolla or Aquamarine crystals if you don't have Turquoise and you can use a combination of these three crystals if you don't have eight of one kind.

WHAT TO DO

1 Lie down comfortably on the floor, using a yoga mat or pad if you prefer.

2 Place six crystals around your body, one above your head, one beneath your feet and two at each side of the body, at the knees and the elbows.

3 Place the seventh crystal underneath your head at the base of the skull and the eighth crystal on your throat.

4 Allow 20 minutes for your body to integrate the energies. Be ready to remove the crystals sooner if your intuition tells you that you have integrated the crystal energy more quickly.

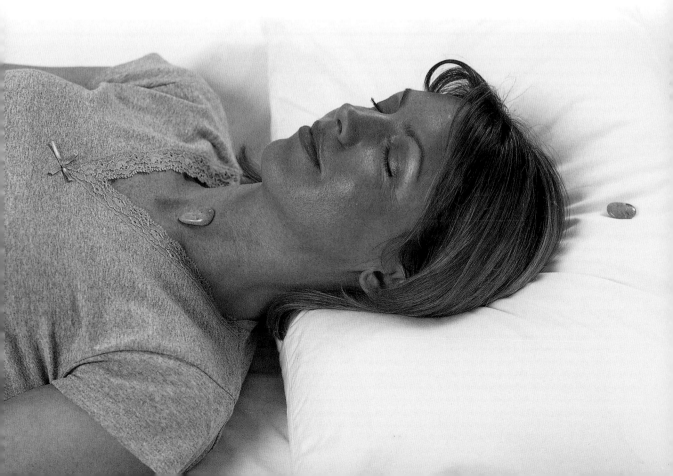

Allergies

If your immune system becomes overly sensitive to a particular substance, you experience an allergic reaction every time you encounter it. This is what happens in hay fever, also known as nasal allergy or allergic rhinitis. Pollens, mould spores, dust, house dust mites and many other airborne substances such as pollution and cigarette smoke are notorious for causing this and other allergic reactions. When you inhale the allergen, the cells in your nasal passage become inflamed, releasing histamine and other chemicals. The physical symptoms are runny nose, postnasal drip, sneezing and itching eyes and nose.

Purification through crystal healing can help you find freedom from the stress and discomfort of allergies. Physically this gem essence helps release excess toxins, fluid and mucus. Emotionally it clears inner conflict caused by past suffering and disappointment. Mentally it brings freedom by releasing exaggerated expectations, especially the manipulative expectations of others. Spiritually it aids 'light body' activation, allowing for a downpouring of soul resonance.

Purification crystals

- Clear Quartz can awaken and balance the chakras or 'inner rainbow'. In esoteric law rainbows are said to bring joy. When your inner rainbow is in balance, your life-force is at its fullest and you are immediately aware of your capacity to enjoy life.

- Danburite clarifies the emotional body by freeing accumulated tears, which may have blocked the flow of heartfelt communication. It is a powerful rejuvenating crystal that with conscious use can clear toxins that cause allergic reactions.

- Morganite opens the heart chakra to deep emotional healing. It quickly releases past suffering caused by illusion and betrayal, and encourages self-love and self-respect. Morganite calms the emotions, so creating a space for you to enjoy life to the full.

Clear Quartz

Danburite

Morganite

Gem essence

This essence is used for purification on all levels. It facilitates change and is a catalyst, heralding freedom on all levels by allowing a change of energy status to happen. It shines a light on the areas of our life where we have disregarded the needs of the soul. It releases torment and obsession caused by too much attention to detail which has caused procrastination.

YOU WILL NEED
1 Clear Quartz, natural or tumbled
1 Danburite, natural or tumbled
1 Morganite, natural or tumbled

WHAT TO DO
Make a combined gem essence (see page 14 for information on how to do this) and take it as directed.

Heart conditions

The physical heart has an intimate connection to every cell in the body. In complementary medicine it is considered to be the balance centre of your body that deals with love and relationships.

The symptoms of the heart condition known as angina are pain or tightness in the chest, arm or jaw that comes on with emotional stress or exertion and subsides with rest. Lifestyle changes such as stopping smoking, losing weight, and reducing stress in your life by practising meditation will greatly enhance your healing potential and improve the quality of your life.

Therapy tip

- You can use Moss Agate or another green crystal if you don't have Aventurine. Green crystals such as Aventurine, Emerald, Malachite, Jade, Bloodstone, Verdelite, Dioptase, Seraphinite, Moss Agate, Moldavite and Peridot all contain the energies of nature which are nurturing and balancing to the subtle-energy systems.

Peridot

Moss Agate

Green Aventurine

Emerald

Balance and freedom

Green crystals generally promote feelings of freedom and space. They can be used to release fear and to remove the tightness in the chest that can become overwhelming when you feel trapped by inharmonious relationships and circumstances. You can use this technique every day to reduce stress.

YOU WILL NEED
6 Green Aventurine, tumbled

WHAT TO DO

1 Lie down comfortably on the floor, using a yoga mat or pad if you prefer.

2 Place three crystals around your body, one just above your head and one beneath each foot. Place one crystal on your heart chakra and hold a crystal in each hand.

3 Relax your body by focussing on your breathing.

4 When you are ready, begin to breathe in the green energies of the crystals. If you find this difficult, just imagine breathing in the colour green.

5 Allow 20 minutes for your body to integrate the energies. Be ready to remove the crystals sooner if your intuition tells you that you have integrated the crystal energy more quickly.

Blood disorders

Besides delivering oxygen to your tissues and removing carbon dioxide, blood carries nutrients, hormones, vitamins, minerals and electrolytes around your body – everything your tissues and organs need to survive.

Blood symbolizes the raw energy of life, which is more than just survival. It is a hyperdynamic superconductor of consciousness that contains the subtle wisdom of your ancestors.

There are a number of disorders that can affect the blood. Some are caused by deficiencies or abnormalities in one of the many different types of blood cells, others by the blood failing to clot or clotting too easily. Some blood disorders are inherited, some caused by nutritional deficiencies, and for some the cause is unknown.

Anaemia is one of the commonest blood disorders. In anaemia there is a problem with haemoglobin, the pigment in red blood cells that carries oxygen around the body. It can be caused by vitamin or mineral deficiencies, such as not enough iron in your diet, or by heavy bleeding. Other causes of anaemia include inherited conditions that affect the production of the red blood cells.

Web of life crystals

- **Magnetite (Lodestone)** is a very important source of iron ore and is excellent for stimulating the blood and circulatory systems. It is a strong grounding and energizing stone that also aligns the spinal column and chakra system. Magnetite aligns our subtle-energy systems with the Earth's magnetic field, bringing security, strength and life-force renewal.

- **Haematite** derives its name from the Greek word for blood, which is descriptive of the colour of one of its forms, the soft powdered mineral red ochre. Ancient superstition held that large deposits of Haematite formed where battles were fought and the blood flowed into the ground, hence its ancient name of 'bloodstone' (not to be confused with the Bloodstone also used in this web — they are different crystals). Haematite is grounding and very energizing, restores equilibrium and stability, supports kidney function, is beneficial to all the fluid functions of the body and is used to staunch bleeding. It purifies and strengthen the blood and aids absorption of iron in the small intestine.

- **Bloodstone**, also known as Heliotrope, has long been valued for its beneficial effects on the heart, blood and circulatory systems. It is used to cleanse the blood of toxins such as mercury, and to stench the flow of blood from wounds. As a gem essence (see page 14) it purifies the blood and detoxifies the organs of elimination as well as supporting the flow of blood and assisting circulation.

Haematite

Magnetite

Bloodstone

Web of life

Repeating this technique often will bring about significant changes as your blood becomes purified and energized. Your natural balance and stability will be renewed and your self-confidence and self-esteem will be boosted. This web connects you to the wisdom of the land, aiding your interconnectedness with the Earth and all sentient life. It heals ancestral miasms (see pages 138–139), removes survival issues and alters fear-based attitudes.

YOU WILL NEED

4 Haematite, tumbled

1 Bloodstone, tumbled

NOTE: You can use Magnetite instead of Haematite, either as natural crystals or in its massive raw form Lodestone.

Therapy tips

- Magnetite and Haematite are very energizing, so do not use this technique just before you go to bed or you will have difficulty sleeping.

- Having a sip of water before a crystal healing session and drinking plenty of water afterwards will ease the removal of toxins and subtle-energetic blocks. These are always released with the integration of new subtle-energy patterns and bio-information.

- It is vital that all crystals are cleansed before and after use (see page 13). This will guarantee that any residual disharmonies are removed from the stones.

WHAT TO DO

1 Lie down comfortably on the floor using a yoga mat or pad if you prefer.

2 Place the four Haematite or Magnetite crystals around you in the shape of a rectangle.

3 Place the Bloodstone on your heart chakra (see page 18 for its location).

4 Allow 20 minutes for your body to integrate the energies. Be ready to remove the crystals sooner if your intuition tells that you have integrated the crystal energy more quickly.

Blood pressure problems

Blood pressure is exactly what it sounds like, the pressure exerted by the blood against the inside of the blood vessels, specifically the arteries. This pressure holds the blood vessels open and keeps the blood flowing to the farthest reaches of the circulatory system. If blood pressure is consistently too high or low, problems may result.

High blood pressure (hypertension) is a common chronic condition, but it can be helped by lifestyle, diet and behavioural changes. Too much pressure causes microscopic damage to the linings of the blood vessels. If left untreated, this can lead to more serious problems such as stroke or heart disease.

Low blood pressure (hypotension) produces symptoms of dizziness and fainting. It may result from shock, or from reduced body fluid volume caused by repeated vomiting, diarrhoea, heavy sweating, untreated diabetes or bleeding. Postural hypotension may be caused by moving from lying to sitting or sitting to standing too quickly.

Gem essence for high blood pressure

Reducing the stress in your life may help control your blood pressure. Blue Lace Agate (also called Avalonite) is soothing, comforting, peaceful and uplifting and can be used anywhere that needs a calming influence. Wearing a pendant of Blue Lace Agate is also highly recommended as it releases feelings of pressure that can lodge in any area of the body, but are normally felt most prominently in the throat area.

YOU WILL NEED

1 Blue Lace Agate, tumbled

WHAT TO DO

Make a gem essence (see page 14 for information on how to do this) and take it as directed.

Blue Lace Agate

Gem essence for low blood pressure

Low blood pressure may be associated with feelings of lethargy and a need for stimulation. The blood and the circulation are a focus of the Ruby vibration. Its deep red ray is seen as raw life-force, prompting the release of adrenaline (epinephrine) into the bloodstream when it is needed, and controlling muscles that give the power to act. It will warm a chilled body, counteract hypothermia and help with anaemia.

YOU WILL NEED

1 Ruby, tumbled

WHAT TO DO

Make a gem essence (see page 14 for information on how to do this) and take it as directed.

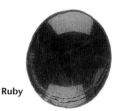

Ruby

Diabetes

There are two major forms of diabetes mellitus. Both have similar symptoms – frequent urination, excessive thirst, weight loss despite unusual hunger, weakness, fatigue, tingling in the hands and feet, reduced resistance to infection and slow healing of cuts. Untreated diabetes can lead to complications such as vision and circulation problems, even impotence, so always remembering to follow you doctor's instructions for managing it is very important.

Diabetes happens when the cells in the body cannot absorb glucose (a type of sugar) properly. In Type I diabetes, which mainly affects children and young people, this is because the pancreas does not produce enough insulin, the hormone needed to regulate blood sugar levels. Insulin injections are needed to control this type, giving it its alternative name of insulin-dependent diabetes. Type II diabetes is sometimes called adult-onset diabetes, because it usually affects people over 40. Surprisingly, at least half the people with the disease are unaware that they have it. It is usually managed by balancing blood sugar levels through medication and diet, giving it yet another alternative name, non-insulin-dependent diabetes.

Craving sugar and sweet foods or comfort eating can be a problem for people with diabetes and for those at risk of developing it. It is a sign that you are seriously undernourished emotionally, Sufferers frequently feel as if all the sweetness has gone out of life, that joy and enthusiasm have vanished. Life feels flat, you may even feel depressed, stressed, have little interest in your physical body and appearance and no libido. You may have frequent mood swings, irritability and PMS (premenstrual syndrome). Sufferers are bound on the spiral of sweetness craving, even though they know they are punishing their bodies beyond all endurance.

Gem essence

Those who crave sugar and other sweet foods need to think pink. All pink crystals will help and Pink Opal in particular in the form of a gem essence will bring relief. Pink Opal (Andean Pink Silica) contains no fire. It has a beneficial effect on the entire endocrine system, releases guilt and teaches you to not to be a victim.

YOU WILL NEED
1 Pink Opal, tumbled

WHAT TO DO
Make a gem essence (see page 14 for information on how to do this) and take it as directed.

Pink Opal

Detoxification

Detoxification of the physical body improves your sense of wellbeing and energy levels. Subtle-body detoxification takes your life to a whole new level of physical, emotional and spiritual wellbeing. In both forms of detox you follow the same core principles.

Danburite medicine

- Use Danburite when you want to bring about change, major or minor, in your life. This crystal allows you to wipe the slate clean, to start again on any level, whether physically, emotionally or spiritually. The energy of pure Danburite will allow you to move on in a new direction, as it carries a very high vibration of the supreme ray of brilliance that clears away blockages in the aura and other subtle bodies. It is also a comforting crystal for those who are making the transition from life to death.

- In everyday use, when worn or carried, Danburite will give a joyful connection to the angelic realms, giving you access to serenity and inner wisdom in your daily encounters. It can facilitate your ability to act with a compassionate heart and an activated mind, guided by the true wisdom of your connection to spirit.

- In meditation Danburite is a powerful aid to the attainment of higher states, because of its natural resonance with the higher frequencies of the human vibrational spectrum.

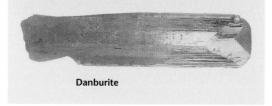

Danburite

Drink 2 litres (3 1/2 pints) of water every day to flush out the toxins that will be released as your body realigns with the new energy patterns.

Eat organic food to reduce the number of chemicals and toxins you ingest, that your body will have to remove one day. Eat simple foods as this helps your body digest them more easily. Keep carbohydrates to a minimum and eat lots of fruit and vegetables.

Rest when you're detoxing and avoid vigorous exercise, instead go walking or practise yoga. Getting to bed early is important as your body needs adequate sleep to regenerate and heal. Sleep restores your body and mind, keeping you mentally alert. It keeps your endocrine and cardiovascular systems functioning and helps ward off disease by strengthening your immune system.

Therapy tips

- Do not apply any pressure; you are relying solely on the energy of the Danburite crystal to do the work for you.

- Never be tempted to dig the crystal into your hand. Instead allow a web of light to be woven around the whole of your hand by just gently touching it with the tip of the crystal.

- Danburite gem essence (see page 14 for information on how to prepare this) is excellent when you want to speed up the detoxification process.

Detoxification treatment

This technique stimulates the main acupuncture meridians in your hands, which encourages positive changes throughout your body. Danburite's crystal energies will gently work through these meridians, releasing any blocked energies and allowing your body to detox.

YOU WILL NEED

1 Danburite, natural

NOTE: For this treatment you need the clear form of Danburite in its natural wand formation with a single termination. The crystal should be about 2–3 cm (1 in) long and 1 cm ($^{1}/2$ in) wide.

WHAT TO DO

1 Begin the treatment on the palm of your left hand.

2 Work the crystal in a gentle rhythmic manner over the whole of your palm from the wrist to the tips of each finger.

3 Then proceed to the back of your hand, working in the same manner.

4 To finish the treatment, go around your hand in the aura (clockwise) direction seven times to seal and protect the energy.

5 Proceed with your other hand in the same manner.

Indigestion

Your digestive system transforms the food you eat into fuel for your body. When it is working harmoniously and you are eating an adequate diet, the energy and nutrients from your food will be absorbed by your bloodstream and carried throughout your body to be used for maintenance and growth. When it is not working harmoniously, you may develop indigestion.

The digestive tract is the part of the digestive system responsible for breaking down food, extracting its nutrients and eliminating the indigestible matter. It consists of the mouth, oesophagus, stomach, small intestine and large intestine. The large intestine, sometimes called the large bowel, includes the colon, rectum and anus. The liver, pancreas and gallbladder are also part of the digestive system. They assist the digestive process by producing important enzymes, hormones and bile, and by storing excess nutrients for later use by the body.

The solar plexus chakra (see page 18) is related to the sun and the element of fire, and governs the process of digestion and the assimilation of nutrients. In relation to the food we ingest, fire can be equated with the many chemical reactions involved in converting that food into fuel for the body. Anger, stress and anxiety overfuel the fire of the solar plexus, causing major imbalance throughout the chakra system and disrupting the harmony of the digestive system.

Fire web crystals

- Amber is detoxifying to the digestive system. It clears tension and anxiety by transmuting negative energy into positive energy.

- Citrine eases digestive disorders and helps with the absorption and assimilation of food. It tones and cleanses the digestive system, which in turn aids the release of toxins and cellulite.

- Peridot dispels negative emotions stored in the heart and solar plexus chakras. It brings youthful renewal, acting as a tonic to spring-clean the whole chakra system.

- Rhodochrosite is a very dynamic crystal with a peach-pink colour-ray. It swiftly clears the sacral, solar plexus and heart chakras of trauma and traumatic events by bringing repressed emotions to the surface to be healed.

- Turquoise is a healer of the emotions of the heart. It encourages heartfelt communication and it supports the energies of the solar plexus chakra and the immune system that increase life energy.

- Lapis (with pyrite inclusions) cleanses, balances and integrates the energies of the throat, solar plexus and crown chakras. This aids the assimilation of nutrients on all levels.

| Amber | Citrine | Peridot | Rhodochrosite | Lapis |

Balancing the fire web

Yellow is the colour associated with the solar plexus chakra, and each of the crystals chosen for this web has a strong yellow component in its colour-ray (even the Lapis contains pyrite inclusions). The solar plexus chakra governs the process of digestion, but we also need to harmonize and balance the other chakras involved in the assimilation of nutrients.

YOU WILL NEED

6 Clear Quartz, with single terminations

1 Amber, natural or tumbled

1 Citrine, natural or tumbled

1 Peridot, natural or tumbled

1 Rhodochrosite, natural or tumbled

1 Turquoise, natural or tumbled

1 Lapis, natural or tumbled

WHAT TO DO

1 Lie down comfortably on the floor, using a yoga mat or pad if you prefer.

2 Place the six Quartz crystals around your body, one above your head, one beneath your feet and two at each side of the body, at the knees and the elbows.

3 Place the other stones as follows: the Amber on your sacral chakra; the Citrine just below your navel; the Peridot at the tip of your sternum (breastbone); the Rhodochrosite on your heart chakra; the Turquoise on your witness point; the Lapis on your throat chakra. The witness point is located on your breastbone between your heart and your throat.

4 Allow 20 minutes for your body to integrate the energies. Be ready to remove the crystals sooner if your intuition tells that you have integrated the crystal energy more quickly.

Bladder problems

The job of your urinary system is to filter out waste products from your blood and excrete them in your urine, and to regulate your body fluid levels. The urinary tract consists of two fist-size kidneys (where the filtration takes place), two ureters that connect the kidneys to the bladder, and a urethra that drains the fluid from the bladder out of the body. At the end of the urethra is a powerful sphincter muscle that holds the urine in until you let your body excrete it.

Cystitis, also known as irritable bladder, is the most common disorder of the urinary tract. Symptoms include pain and a burning sensation during urination, and a frequent urge to urinate, often without passing much urine. The urine may be cloudy or reddish in colour, and have a strong odour. There may also be pain, aching or discomfort in the pubic area or back; fever; fatigue and occasionally nausea and vomiting. Cystitis is usually caused by a bladder or urinary tract infection (UTI). Although anyone can get cystitis it is more common in women, as the female urethra is much shorter than the male. This allows bacteria to reach the bladder more quickly. Left untreated, the infection can spread up to the kidneys. Drinking plenty of water or cranberry juice to help flush the system are safe preventative measures.

The hot, scalding, burning sensations of cystitis relate to emotions that are brought about by unhealthy relationships. These are the relationships that have held you back, made you feel guilty or blocked your creative flow, causing you to perhaps feel despair and lose your joy for life. Betrayal and deception block feelings of joy and regeneration.

Regeneration web

The watery sacral chakra (see page 18) governs the fluid functions of the body. The colour that relates to the sacral chakra is orange. All orange-coloured crystals encourage creativity, activity, detoxification, movement and the flow of communication between the mind and the body. They cleanse and heal emotional wounds, especially suppressed emotions. In this web the work of the orange Carnelians is supported by the high intensity blue Lapis.

YOU WILL NEED

3 Lapis, tumbled

3 Carnelian, tumbled

NOTE: You could use Zincite instead of Carnelian, and Blue Sapphire or Siberian Blue Quartz instead of Lapis.

WHAT TO DO

1 Lie down comfortably on the floor, using a yoga mat or pad if you prefer.

2 Place one Lapis at the top of your head, one at base of your throat, and one just below and beneath your feet.

3 Place one Carnelian on your sacral chakra, and the other two at the groin points on the front of your hips.

4 Allow 20 minutes for your body to integrate the energies. Be ready to remove the crystals sooner if your intuition tells that you have integrated the crystal energy more quickly.

Regeneration web crystals

- Carnelian's signature is strong, stimulating and protective. It is used to repair the etheric body after shock, trauma, loss or betrayal. It ameliorates grief, including the grief associated with bereavement. It enhances creativity and optimism and induces a positive outlook on life. It eases fears and phobias by balancing the body's energy levels.

- Lapis is a high-intensity etheric stone that sedates the conscious mind and is therefore good for relaxation. It gives relief from physical pain and helps with self-expression.

- Zincite enhances life-force, as well as bringing confidence, strength, creativity and courage. It provides for the synergy of personal power, freedom, strength and endurance in all endeavours. If you are feeling pessimistic, are dwelling on past events, depressed, or in shock, then Zincite is a very good crystal to work with. It helps you let go of the past, of painful memories, shock, trauma, psychological paralysis and the fear of moving forward.

- Blue Sapphire and Siberian Blue Quartz relieve stress, release emotional bondage and give relief from physical pain. They allow you to go beyond your self-limiting belief system into the energy of joy and renewal.

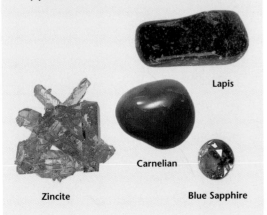

Lapis

Carnelian

Zincite

Blue Sapphire

Back problems

Back pain is a common health problem. Acute back pain may be caused by a pull or strain on a muscle or ligament, perhaps as the result of lifting something heavy. Persistent back pain is often due to postural problems, caused by standing, sitting or sleeping with the spine out of alignment.

More serious causes of back pain are less common. Scoliosis is a sideways curvature of the spine that may affect children. A herniated or prolapsed intervertebral disc ('slipped disc') causes severe pain and can result from an injury or a fall. It is also related to ageing, because as you age, your intervertebral disks start to dry out, making them more likely to herniate.

The spine does not only support your physical body, it is also the support system of your whole psyche. On the emotional level, you may not feel supported by your family, friends or colleagues at work.

Therapy tip

- You can use these crystals to practise spinal alignment with a friend or partner. Use a single Magnetite, Boji stone® or Haematite crystal and move it slowly up their back 2–3 cm (1 in) above their spine. Allowing your intuition to guide you, hold the crystal over any painful or congested areas. Boji stones® hold a balanced polarity so you can use just one on an acupuncture or acupressure point.

Female Boji stone®

Male Boji stone®

Spinal alignment

You can choose from three types of crystal when using this technique to work on the alignment of your spine. Magnetite (Lodestone) aligns the spinal column and releases pain. Haematite restores equilibrium and stability by swiftly removing energy blockages. Boji stones® are used for tissue regeneration and pain removal. Use your intuition to guide you in your choice.

YOU WILL NEED

2 Magnetite, natural

OR

2 Boji stones® (pair of 1 male and 1 female)

OR

2 Haematite, tumbled

WHAT TO DO

1 Lie down comfortably on the floor, using a yoga mat or pad if you prefer.

2 Place one Magnetite or Haematite or Boji stone® at the base of your spine and the other at the base of your skull.

3 Allow 20 minutes for your body to restructure and integrate the energies. Remove the crystals sooner if your intuition tells that you have integrated the crystal energy more quickly.

Nervous system problems

All our voluntary and involuntary actions, our thoughts and feelings, our senses and our body processes are controlled by our nervous systems. The immense complexity of the system means that it can be affected by a wide range of ailments.

The brain and spinal cord together form the central nervous system (CNS), which processes and coordinates nerve signals. These signals are transmitted to and from the CNS by the peripheral nervous system, which consists of all the nerves that branch out from the CNS to all the other parts of the body. Together these systems are responsible for the information we receive from our senses and everything we do by choice. The autonomic nervous system is responsible for controlling those body functions that we think of as happening automatically, such as breathing, digestion, sweating, heartbeat and so on.

Therapy tip

- **Use Citrine and Amethyst to make Ametrine gem essence (see page 14 for information on how to prepare this). It will integrate the solar plexus chakra with the crown chakra and so strengthen concentration and aid analytical skills.**

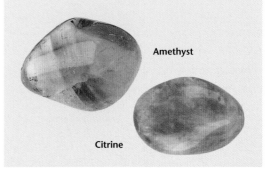

Amethyst

Citrine

Clarity web

The complexity of the nervous system can lead to confused and incoherent thought. In this web, Citrine calms your nervous system, bringing clarity to your thought processes, while Amethyst releases agitation and stress and so aids coherent thought.

YOU WILL NEED
5 Citrine, tumbled
3 Amethyst, tumbled

WHAT TO DO

1 Lie down comfortably on the floor, using a yoga mat or pad if you prefer.

2 Place the five Citrine crystals around your body, one beneath your feet and two at each side of your body at your knees and your elbows.

3 Place the first Amethyst underneath your head at the base of the skull, the second above your head and the third on your third eye chakra (see page 18 for the location of your chakras).

4 Allow 20 minutes for your body to integrate the energies. Be ready to remove the crystals sooner if your intuition tells that you have integrated the crystal energy more quickly.

Pain

Pain anywhere in the body is an indication that there is something wrong. Once you know the cause, it is useful to be able to bring the pain down to an acceptable level. This is especially true for chronic pain, where analgesics have been prescribed for long-term use. Such persistent pain may be influence by mental and emotional factors, as well as the original physical cause.

Pain is concentrated energy that needs defusing so that balance can be restored. If you scan the painful area with your hand, you may be aware of subtle-energy changes. Painful concentrated energy feels sticky, prickly, spiky or congested. When the pain has been removed, the area will often feel buoyant or smooth to the touch.

The crystal healing technique used for pain relief may be the most important and useful technique you will ever learn to use. It can be used to draw out any imbalanced energy or subtle-energy blockages, not just pain. This technique can be used over meridians, chakras and on any area of the physical body or aura, and can be repeated as many times as needed.

Unwinding pain

Smoky Quartz draws discordant energy towards itself and absorbs it. This technique uses Smoky Quartz to unwind the painful concentrated energy, followed by Clear Quartz to place healing energy in. The clearer the Quartz crystal, the faster the energy will flow. Before you begin, make sure that you and anyone you are working with (if you are using this technique on someone else) are fully centred, grounded, focused and balanced.

YOU WILL NEED

1 Smoky Quartz, 10–15 cm (4–6 in) long, with single termination

1 Clear Quartz, 10–15 cm (4–6 in) long, with single termination

NOTE: You may use an Obsidian sphere instead of the Smoky Quartz crystal. It should be 6 cm (2½ in) in diameter and fit comfortably into your hand.

WHAT TO DO

1 Hold the Smoky Quartz crystal in your left hand with the termination pointing at the painful area. Remove the concentrated energies by moving the crystal just above the area in an anticlockwise (unwinding) direction. Continue until your intuition tells you that you have removed as much concentrated painful energy as possible, or until the pain has substantially decreased or gone altogether.

2 Change hands and change crystal. Hold the Clear Quartz crystal in your right hand with the termination pointing at the painful area. Place the healing energy in, working in a clockwise (winding) direction. Place as much healing energy in as possible; your intuition will tell you when the process is complete.

3 To finish sweep your Clear Quartz crystal sideways over the area. This encourages the energy to begin flowing smoothly.

4 Wash your hands in cold water to release any unwanted energies. Cold water does not open your pores and therefore it protects you from absorbing the energy you have just released.

5 Cleanse the crystals after use (see page 13).

Therapy tips

- The size of the crystals you use for this technique is very important. The bigger the crystal the better, but do not choose one so big that it makes your arm ache, or you will quickly tire. Laser wands (see page 10) are very suitable.

- Other types of Quartz can be used to enhance this technique. For pain due to an injury, place a Quartz crystal on each side of the injured area with the terminations facing each other. Rutile Quartz can also be used to speed tissue repair.

- To relieve physical pain such as that of arthritis or menstrual discomfort, place an Amethyst or Smoky Quartz crystal over the affected area.

- Boji stones® can also used to draw out pain.

Smoky Quartz

Clear Quartz

Arthritis

Arthritis is the name given to a number of conditions that cause inflamed, painful, stiff and swollen joints. Typically it strikes the knees, hips, knuckles and spine. The initial symptoms are often just twinges of stiffness, but ultimately these can lead to persistent pain, stiffness, loss of flexibility, or swelling in affected joints.

Osteoarthritis is the most common type of arthritis. It mostly affects people aged 45 and over, particularly postmenopausal women. It is classified as a degenerative bone disease because it is the result of cartilage deterioration. Cartilage is the smooth, slippery cushion on the ends of bones where they meet at the joints. It provides protection to the bones and reduces friction during movement. Its deterioration may be due to wear and tear, diet, stress or injury to the affected joint, or an inherited tendency to osteoarthritis.

Rheumatoid arthritis is an auto-immune disease that affects three times more women than men, again mostly aged 45 or older. It can affect most joints of the body, and they may become severely deformed. While it essentially attacks the joint lining or synovial membrane, it can also affect the body in other ways, causing weakness, fatigue, loss of appetite, anaemia, muscle pain and weight loss.

Less common forms of arthritis include gout, lupus and ankylosing spondylitis. Children may be affected by various types of juvenile rheumatoid arthritis.

Copper's reputation for bringing relief to arthritis sufferers by reducing inflammation and increasing flexibility is well known. It may be worn as a bracelet, necklace or ring or, as here, used in an energy web.

It is also important as a trace element in your diet. Copper is concentrated in your liver, heart, brain, kidneys and hair. It helps your body absorb and use iron, is important for vitamin C metabolism and helps balance cholesterol levels. Because it forms part of many enzymes, it is essential for many of your body's functions: making energy from your food; maintaining healthy myelin (which forms the sheath surrounding nerve fibres); producing melanin (a skin and hair pigment); bone development; and maintaining a healthy reproductive system and immune system.

Copper-rich crystals

- Malachite is formed when copper ores in the ground are dissolved and subsequently deposited in cavities and veins in rocks. Chemically, it is primarily a hydrated copper carbonate. On a physical level it alleviates rheumatism and helps reduce acidification of the tissues. It is a diagnostic crystal that quickly gets to the heart of the problem. With dedicated use it can balance and bring harmony to the body.

- Dioptase works primarily on the thymus and immune system. It reduces inflammation and speeds up detoxification. Chemically it is a copper silicate and has a likeness to Chrysocolla. A beautiful deep blue-green crystal, it is not common but is found in oxidized parts of copper sulphate deposits.

- Chrysocolla cleanses and energizes all the body systems and is especially useful for stimulating the immune system. It forms from solutions of silica, water and copper.

- Turquoise strengthens and support the immune system and is used to alleviate arthritis. Chemically it is a hydrated phosphate of aluminium and copper.

Flexibility web

Copper is not only beneficial in arthritis, but it is such a great conductor of energy that it brings harmony to the body's many energy systems. The Clear Quartz crystals in this energy web are used to amplify and direct the flow of the copper crystal.

NOTE: Nuggets of copper are widely available, but you could use copper-rich crystals such as Dioptase, Malachite, Chrysocolla or Turquoise instead.

YOU WILL NEED
1 Copper nugget
2 Clear Quartz, with single terminations

WHAT TO DO

1 Lie down comfortably on the floor, using a yoga mat or pad if you prefer.

2 Place the Copper nugget on your heart chakra (see page 18 for its location).

3 Hold a Clear Quartz crystal in each hand. Have the termination pointing inwards in your left hand and outwards in your right hand.

4 Allow 20 minutes for your body to integrate the energies. Be ready to remove the crystals sooner if your intuition tells that you have integrated the crystal energy more quickly.

Skin complaints

Many different factors affect the health of your skin. Digestive imbalances, food allergies, nutritional deficiencies, toxic liver, chemicals, exposure to the weather, even age, will all show their effects on the skin of your face and body. Ultraviolet rays from the sun or sunbeds are particularly hard on the skin. Physical changes to the body, such as having a baby or losing weight, can cause stretchmarks.

As you get older, your skin naturally loses elasticity as the connective tissue in the deepest layer begins to deteriorate. Elastin and collagen, protein substances that keep skin toned and pliable, are gradually depleted. The result is skin that thins, wrinkles, sags, becomes drier and may bruise more easily.

Premature ageing of the skin is associated with damage caused by pollution, poor diet, too much ultraviolet light, alcohol and smoking. Small hyperpigmented areas may also develop on the skin. These are known as age spots or liver spots.

Acne mostly affects young skin, but sometimes also occurs in adults. The oil-producing sebaceous glands in the skin become blocked, infected and inflamed. Blackheads, whiteheads, spots and pimples are all associated with acne. In severe cases there may be larger inflamed areas of skin, deep cyst formation and resulting scarring. Hormonal imbalances and poor diet may be responsible.

In eczema and dermatitis the skin becomes itchy, dry, blistered and thickened because of an allergic reaction. The trigger may be food or drug sensitivity. Other causes include contact with external irritants and allergens such as chemicals, cleaning products, synthetic fabrics, cosmetics or nickel in jewellery. These conditions are often associated with migraine, poor immune system function and with other allergies such as asthma, hay fever and urticaria.

Psoriasis also produces itchy, thickened skin but is not caused by an allergy. The exact cause is unknown, but the condition is not contagious. It normally affects the scalp, elbows, knees and the backs of hands, but can affect any body area. The red scaly patches can be painful as well as itchy. Symptoms worsen with stress or toxic overload.

In rosacea the skin of the face develops permanent or sporadic redness or flushing, caused by the swelling of blood vessels under the skin. It may be caused by excess alcohol, skin infections, digestive imbalances or an autoimmune disease.

Facial massage

We tend to be especially careful in looking after our facial skin, because it is often the first thing that people notice. A facial massage improves circulation, making your skin look fresher and more glowing. It also relaxes the facial muscles, which releases tension frowns and furrows. The choice of crystals for this massage is influenced by the fact that our emotions also affect our faces. Rose Quartz is a primary emotional healing crystal that can help skin conditions that have an emotional stress trigger, while Moonstone is soothing and comforting to the emotions.

YOU WILL NEED

1 Moonstone, tumbled

OR

1 Rose Quartz, tumbled

WHAT TO DO

1 Cleanse your face, taking care not to drag the skin.

2 Apply a light oil of your choice to your facial skin to encourage a more fluid movement of the crystal.

3 Using small circular movements, gently massage your face and neck with the crystal. Start on your neck and move up to your chin area, then work around your mouth, cheeks and nose. Massage the area around your eyes very gently indeed. Finish by massaging your forehead.

4 Rest the palms of your hands on your face with your fingertips touching your forehead and the heels of your hands on your chin. Press very gently and slowly draw your hands towards your ears. Repeat this movement three times.

Therapy tips

- Make a Rose Quartz gem essence (see page 14 for information on how to do this) and take it internally or dilute it and use it on your skin. This essence can be added to aqueous cream or any other plain skin cream or lotion, and simply smoothed into the skin. It can also be added to a carrier oil such as sweet almond, apricot kernel, grapeseed or jojoba oils and then massaged into the skin. Adding frankincense to the carrier oil will also help the skin to have a youthful appearance.

- Adding a few drops of frankincense essential oil and a Rose Quartz or Moonstone tumbled stone to your bath will rejuvenate your whole body.

- Skin conditions can be aggravated by stress. Wearing a Moonstone pendant helps to balance not only the emotions but the fluid systems of the body as well.

Rose Quartz

Moonstone

Cellulite

Cellulite is fatty tissue that forms on the backs of legs, buttocks, thighs, hips and upper arms. Excess oestrogen and poor blood circulation may cause toxins, fat and fluid to get trapped in pockets under the skin. The typical 'orange peel' dimples of cellulite become more noticeable with age. Massage, a healthy diet, exercise and body brushing will all help to reduce the appearance of cellulite.

Therapy tips

- Adding a few drops of a gem essence or essential oil to the carrier oil will make it even more effective. Citrine or Iolite gem essence will help to rid the body of toxins and cellulite. Patchouli, juniperberry and sweet orange are detoxifying essential oils.

- Massage is a very safe technique, but there are times and conditions when it should be avoided. Often this just means avoiding a body area, but use your common sense. Do not massage just after eating a heavy meal; a person with a raised temperature; any infected area, swelling or inflammation; over an area where varicose veins are present; or bruised or broken skin.

Clear Quartz sphere

Crystal massage

Massage is suitable for everyone and is beneficial in several ways. It improves blood circulation, calms the nervous system, stimulates and tones the skin, improves muscle tone, eases aches and pains in muscles and joints, and can help ease fluid retention. It is also possible to use this massage technique on your aura. This is energetically effective and suitable for broken or bruised skin.

YOU WILL NEED
1 Clear Quartz massage wand

NOTE If you do not have a massage wand, you can use a very large tumbled Clear Quartz stone, sphere or egg instead. Do not choose a crystal that is so big that it makes your arm ache, or you will quickly tire.

WHAT TO DO

1 Smooth a carrier oil of your choice onto your body to help the crystal glide easily over your skin. Carrier oils such as sweet almond, apricot kernel, grapeseed or jojoba are suitable.

2 Use the crystal to massage your body with small circular clockwise movements. You may wish to massage your whole body, or just the problem areas. Experiment with the amount of pressure you apply, making sure it always feels comfortable.

Yeast infections

We have 2 kg (4½ lb) of bacteria (gut flora) in our digestive tract. Usually there is a balance between the 'good' and the 'bad' bacteria, and this balance is essential for our health. Good bacteria (often called 'friendly' bacteria or probiotics) are easily killed by antibiotics. Once this happens, the bad bacteria, moulds and yeasts such as *Candida albicans* can flourish to such an extent that they take over the gut environment and produce toxic substances. Friendly bacteria keep these pathogens (disease-causing agents) down and help stimulate growth of the gut lining.

Although *Candida albicans* is a yeast that occurs naturally in the body, it can cause problems if it multiplies too rapidly. Taking antibiotics and not eating a healthy balanced diet increase the risk of *Candida* overgrowth, sometimes called candidiasis or thrush.

Symptoms vary depending on which parts of the body are affected. Vaginal thrush causes itching and redness, and a cottage-cheese-like discharge. If the digestive system is affected, then symptoms can include bloating, fatigue, sugar cravings, headaches, anal itching, leaky gut, irritability, joint pains,

Smoky Quartz medicine

- Smoky Quartz helps you to develop a strong healthy body and a calm, peaceful, stress-free mind. It eases despair and suicidal tendencies. It relieves headaches and congestion of the intestines.

Smoky Quartz

recurrent sore throats, halitosis and sensitivity to chemicals. *Candida albicans* infection may lead to emotional instability and lack of mental focus, especially when it can bring on so many apparently unrelated health problems.

Gem essence

A balanced lifestyle that includes good dietary habits is vital if you wish to achieve a healthy, happy, productive life. Smoky Quartz is particularly useful when your body's energy systems are out of control. It can focus and ground internal energy that has become unstable, absorb stagnant disruptive energy and helps you to find the balance you need.

YOU WILL NEED
1 Smoky Quartz, tumbled

WHAT TO DO
Make a gem essence (see page 14 for information on how to do this) and take it as directed.

Sexual dysfunction

Low libido (decreased sex drive) is the persistent loss of interest in sex to below the level that you consider normal for you. Your libido can be depleted for a multitude of reasons including stress, fatigue, depression, hormonal imbalances, menopause, an underactive thyroid or insufficient blood flow to the sexual organs.

Impotence (erectile dysfunction) is the persistent inability to achieve or maintain an erection, and is most commonly caused by a combination of physical and psychological factors. Physical factors include alcoholism, hormone imbalances, prostrate disorders, diabetes, high blood pressure and certain medications. Stress, depression, anxiety and personal problems with a sexual partner are among the psychological causes.

Ruby medicine

- Ruby regulates blood, circulation and adrenaline (epinephrine) release into the bloodstream as well as the reproductive system. It warms the body, stops chills, and eases stiff muscles in the feet, legs, knees and hips.

- The dynamism of Ruby removes fear and worries about survival, and restores the will to live. It detoxes by removing inertia, increases physical energy and can be used if you are feeling tired.

Ruby

Improving your sexuality

Ruby signifies and arouses lust, and governs the genitals and reproductive organs. You can use its raw power to release energy blocks deep within you. Ruby activates, vitalizes, intensifies and increases desire. It utilizes infrared, the slowest vibration of the colour spectrum, and gives a new boost to processes that have been sluggish or stagnant.

YOU WILL NEED
8 Ruby crystals, tumbled

WHAT TO DO
1 Lie down comfortably on the floor, using a yoga mat or pad if you prefer.

2 Place six crystals around your body, one above your head, one beneath your feet and two at each side of your body, at your knees and your elbows.

3 Place the seventh crystal underneath your head at the base of your skull and the eighth crystal on your heart chakra (see page 18).

4 Allow 20 minutes for your body to integrate the energies. Be ready to remove the crystals sooner if your intuition tells that you have integrated the crystal energy more quickly.

Infertility

Infertility may be defined as the failure to conceive a child after a year of regular, unprotected sexual intercourse.

Lifestyle choices and environmental conditions may be contributory factors in infertility in both sexes. A poor diet, being overweight or underweight, smoking, alcohol, stress, and occupational and environmental exposure to certain chemicals and pesticides can all have an effect. Sexually transmitted infections (STIs) such as gonorrhoea in men and chlamydia in women (which often goes undetected) are also major causes of infertility.

In men other contributory factors that can affect the quality and mobility of sperm include wearing tight underwear, sitting in hot baths or tubs, environmental oestrogens in plastics and tap water, and prostrate disorders. In women, physical problems that may lead to infertility include hormonal imbalance, blocked fallopian tubes, failure to ovulate, uterine fibroids, a past ectopic pregnancy, endometriosis, pelvic inflammatory disease (PID), polycystic ovary syndrome (PCOS), thyroid problems and vaginal overacidity. Extreme dieting and excessive exercise can also be factors.

Carnelian medicine

- Carnelian has a strong influence over the female reproductive system. It releases stress and trauma that has damaged the etheric body. Carnelian restores vitality, stimulates creativity and improves the energy flow within the physical body.

Carnelian

Creative fire

Treatment for infertility depends on its cause, and can be expensive, frustrating and costly. If no cause for infertility is found this crystal healing technique can clear subtle-energetic pathways, which may help conception.

YOU WILL NEED
6 Clear Quartz, with single terminations
2 Carnelian, tumbled

WHAT TO DO

1 Lie down comfortably on the floor, using a yoga mat or pad if you prefer.

2 Place six Clear Quartz crystals around your body, one above your head, one beneath your feet and two at each side of your body, at the knees and the elbows. The terminations should point outwards.

3 Place one Carnelian on your sacral chakra (just below the navel) and one at your witness point. The witness point is located on your breastbone between your heart and your throat.

4 Allow 20 minutes for your body to integrate the energies. Be ready to remove the crystals sooner, if your intuition tells that you have integrated the crystal energy more quickly.

Menstrual problems

PMS (premenstrual syndrome) affects some women for up to two weeks before the start of their menstrual period. It has a multitude of symptoms, both physical and emotional. Physical problems may include bloating, headache, weight gain, breast tenderness, food cravings, fatigue, acne, changes in bowel habits, hot flushes, insomnia, nausea and dizziness. Irritability, anxiety, depression, mood swings, nervousness, anger, confusion, trouble concentrating and memory loss are among the emotional symptoms. Imbalances in hormone levels, gut flora and blood sugar levels may be contributory causes, as may nutrient deficiencies, food intolerances, stress and less than optimum liver function.

Water (fluid) retention can also occur before a period or during the menopause. Hormonal imbalance, stress and food intolerances may again be contributory factors, and so may insulin resistance, excessive salt consumption, low fluid intake, obesity, high blood pressure and heart problems.

In dysmenorrhoea (painful menstrual periods), cramps in the lower abdomen may be intermittent or constant, and there may also be lower back pain. Headaches, nausea and vomiting affect some women.

Heavy or irregular periods can affect all women at menstruation time, especially while going through the menopause. Hormone imbalance and weight gain are contributory factors.

The area of the body affected by all these problems is the pelvic region. The pelvis is shaped like a bowl, it holds our vital life-force (*chi*) and is related to the element of water. It is governed by the sacral chakra (see page 18 for its location).

The sacral chakra governs the flow of energy between your body and your emotions. Stress blocks this communication and throws your body out of balance. Pain in this centre that is held onto and not released will cause stagnation and rigidity on all levels, not just the physical.

The crescent moon is the sacral chakra's symbol. The moon has a powerful influence over water and the female reproductive cycle is controlled by the phases of the moon. Because the moon is part hidden and portrayed as a crescent, it gives the feeling of the *yin/yang* balance required to manifest awareness of the female liquid emotional energy within the body.

Moonstone medicine

- Moonstone appears mysterious and magical, with a ghostly shimmering glow floating in a crystalline material. Throughout the ages, people have celebrated the role of the goddess in maintaining balance and harmony, and Moonstone is her talisman.

- Through its close association with lunar energies, Moonstone facilitates deep understanding and celebration of the cycles and tides of life, the ebb and flow of birth, death and regeneration.

- Moonstone is nurturing to the soul and heals the subtle-energy system by comforting and aiding serene contemplation.

Moonstone

Breathing balance

The female creative force is mysterious and powerful. Working with crystal breathing techniques allows women to explore this chakra's feminine creative nature and balance. Morganite and Moonstone are both suitable stones for this technique, Morganite because it works on the female reproductive system, Moonstone because it is the female power stone.

YOU WILL NEED

1 Morganite, tumbled

OR

1 Moonstone, tumbled

WHAT TO DO

1 Sit in a comfortable position and allow your body to relax for a few minutes.

2 Hold the crystal in your hands in front of you. Gently gaze at it and relax your body by focussing on your breathing.

3 When you are ready allow your eyes to close and begin to breathe in the energies of the crystal you are holding.

4 You can continue with this breathing technique for as long as you feel comfortable.

Morganite medicine

- Morganite's signature is very special. As we begin to truly heal, we find our emotions are volatile, because healing sometimes brings up painful memories. It is easy to get swamped and give up rather than having the courage to go with the flow. Morganite holds the emotional body stable as you let go of the pain and this is the key to its use.

Morganite

Menopause

Menopause, the time when menstrual periods cease, is the end of a woman's reproductive years. The hormonal changes that take place around the menopause have different effects on different women. Although most have few or no problems at all, others suffer severely.

Hot flushes are the symptom most associated with the menopause. The face, neck or body become hot and red and perspiration increases. This is followed by a faster heart beat, and sometimes nausea and tingling in the hands. Hot flushes can occur at any time of the day or night and can cause sleep disturbances.

Other symptoms associated with the menopause include vaginal dryness, thinning of the vaginal lining, falling libido, headache, migraine, thyroid imbalance, weight gain, water retention, disrupted sleep, fatigue, stress, depression, memory loss, poor concentration, mood swings, lack of self-confidence and panic attacks. Menstrual periods may become heavy or irregular before they finally stop.

Some women also find the menopause coincides with their children leaving home. For many women their children are the centre of their universe and entering the territory of the 'empty-nesters' can make them feel very wobbly emotionally.

Women of all ages need to focus on their dreams and personal ambitions. That way whatever age you are you will increase your self-confidence and self-esteem. Remember that what you get out of life is more to do with attitude than age. A healthy attitude is particularly important during the menopause, when it is essential to balance your hormones, eat a healthy diet, take regular exercise and take up relaxation or yoga.

Menopause is also a great time to develop new interests and take stock of your life. After the menopause, many women develop a new body awareness or body intelligence that takes them beyond the limiting patterns of the physical. More and more women see the menopause as a time of great personal growth, power and initiation to a true 'change of life'.

Body intelligence web crystals

- **Clear Quartz** crystals placed around the body unify the subtle-energy field and attract positive life-force. This allows for a clearer understanding of the many changes taking place on all levels of the psyche.

- **Smoky Quartz** on the root chakra gives grounding, stability and anchoring qualities. These help the physical body cope with the changes taking place, which can sometimes feel like being cast adrift on an 'ocean of change'.

- **Carnelian** balances the sacral chakra and brings the energy of joy and spontaneity.

- **Malachite** balances the solar plexus chakra and helps with the development of personal willpower.

- **Morganite** balances the heart chakra and holds the emotional body stable as changes unfold.

- **Lapis** balances the throat chakra and helps with self-expression and self-esteem.

- **Tanzanite** balances the third eye chakra giving insight and inspiration.

Body intelligence web

Although the sacral chakra governs the reproductive organs, we need to harmonize and balance all the chakra centres because the effects of the menopause can influence the whole body. This technique produces a synergy affect which focuses and amplifies the potency of all the crystals.

YOU WILL NEED

6 Clear Quartz, with single terminations

1 Smoky Quartz, tumbled

1 Carnelian, tumbled

1 Malachite, tumbled

1 Morganite, tumbled

1 Lapis, tumbled

1 Tanzanite, tumbled

WHAT TO DO

1 Lie down comfortably on the floor, using a yoga mat or pad if you prefer.

2 Place the six Clear Quartz crystals around your body, one above your head, one beneath your feet and two at each side of your body, at the knees and the elbows.

3 Place the Smoky Quartz on your root chakra, the Carnelian on your sacral chakra, the Malachite on your solar plexus chakra, the Morganite on your heart chakra, the Lapis on your throat chakra and the Tanzanite on your third eye chakra (see page 18 for chakra locations).

4 Relax your body by focussing on your breathing.

5 Allow 20 minutes for your body to integrate the energies. Be ready to remove the crystals sooner if your intuition tells that you have integrated the crystal energy more quickly.

Osteoporosis

Bone is a living tissue, and as such is constantly being broken down and reabsorbed by the body and then built up again. During childhood, new bone is built up faster than it is broken down. This process continues until peak bone density is reached, usually in early adulthood. After that, the bone breakdown process accelerates and the bone replacement process slows down.

Osteoporosis, meaning porous (porosis) bone (osteo), occurs when too much bone is broken down and is inadequately replaced. As people grow older, their bones gradually become thinner, lighter and more porous. Consequently, they weaken, become more brittle and more likely to break. A fracture is often the first sign of the condition, but doctors can take bone mineral density measurements to predict the likelihood of osteoporosis developing.

Although osteoporosis is a natural part of ageing, the severity of its effects varies considerably. Poor nutrition, anorexia, excessive weight loss, early menopause, hysterectomy, certain medications and medical conditions, excessive alcohol, smoking and hormonal imbalances (especially after the menopause) can all make matters worse.

Preventative treatment for osteoporosis should really begin when you are in your thirties. However, it is never to late to start: eat foods high in calcium and vitamin D; take regular weight-bearing exercise; stop smoking; limit your alcohol consumption; and correct any hormonal imbalances.

Gem essence

Amazonite is often recommended for osteoporosis, tooth decay, calcium absorption and muscle spasms. Blue to green in colour, it is soothing to the nervous system and aligns the etheric body with the physical body. It has a beneficial influence on the throat and heart chakras and is often used to activate and balance the thymus gland, which lies midway between these two chakra points.

YOU WILL NEED
1 Amazonite, tumbled

WHAT TO DO
Make a gem essence (see page 14 for information on how to do this) and take it as directed.

Amazonite

Weight problems

Being overweight brings an increased risk of developing serious diseases, including high blood pressure, heart disease, stroke, diabetes and arthritis. It may also cause low self-esteem and depression.

Weight gain can occur as we get older, especially around the menopause. A little weight gain is acceptable but an excessive increase is unhealthy. Sugar cravings, poor balance of blood sugar levels, an underactive thyroid, water retention, hormone imbalance, overeating and insufficient exercise can all contribute. Keeping hormone levels in balance plays an important role in weight control, especially around the menopause.

The theory of losing weight is simple, just eat fewer calories than usual and burn off more through increased exercise. Unfortunately this isn't as easy as it sounds! More aggressive dieting leads to a lifelong cycle of weight loss and gain that, in the end, leaves people more overweight than they would have been if they had never dieted.

Therapy tip

- Drink plenty of water. It aids digestion and helps you feel full, as well as assisting in the release of toxins.

Iolite

Being too thin can also cause health problems. Overly thin women and those who suffer from anorexia are more prone to osteoporosis after the menopause. Frail elderly people have less resistance to pneumonia, influenza and other illnesses.

Gem essence

Iolite assists in lessening fatty deposits in the body and in releasing toxins. Metaphysically, fatty deposits are linked to stored negative emotions and toxins to old belief systems. Iolite will allow you to see your true potential rather than society's expectations and stereotyping. It also alleviates addictions, as it allows us to understand what addiction is and why we have developed a craving for a certain food, substance, situation or person.

YOU WILL NEED
1 Iolite, tumbled

WHAT TO DO
Make a gem essence (see page 14 for information on how to do this) and take it as directed.

Ageing

Allowing for genetic differences, the state of our health as we grow older depends to a large degree on how well we take care of ourselves. A healthy diet and regular exercise improve our chances of thriving in our later years.

Although minor slowing of reflexes, thinking and memory appears to be a normal outcome of ageing, senility is not. Memory or concentration loss can occur at any age, and may be symptoms of inadequate blood supply to the brain, nutrient deficiencies, stress or imbalanced hormones.

Many people worry that any lapse of memory is an early symptom of Alzheimer's disease, a form of dementia. Although confusion, forgetfulness, depression, and irritability are early symptoms of Alzheimer's, nine out of ten people with those problems will not have the disease. Poor nutrition and digestion, brain toxins, poor circulation and genetics may all contribute to dementia.

If you become aware of the connection between your breath, your nervous system and your brain, you will have a tool with which to enhance all areas of your life. This will help you maintain optimum health, vitality and balance. Because breathing is such a fundamental process in our survival, we always take its power for granted. We do not have to think about the process of breathing because it is governed by the autonomic nervous system. We assume we will just do it anyway.

In fact the physical function of breathing is far more than just breathing in and out. Inhalation (breathing in) carries the life-force, also known as *chi* or *prana*. When you are stressed, tense, angry or fearful, your breathing is short, fast and shallow. When you are peaceful and relaxed your breath is long, slow and deep and charged with the life-force. When you breathe fully and deeply your chest expands, assisting the release of inner tensions and toxins as you exhale.

Therapy tips

- This exercise is quite quick and is performed seated, so it can be done anywhere and at any time.

- It is a potent exercise and should be done in moderation at first. Performed regularly over time it can enhance your vitality, help to reduce your stress levels and improve your memory function.

- Use it often to restore vitality, reduce stress and aid relaxation.

Clear Quartz

Crystal breathing

Increasing your vitality through conscious breathing exercises can improve overall feelings of wellbeing whatever your age. Using a Clear Quartz crystal to support the entire process will naturally increase your life-force.

YOU WILL NEED

1 large Clear Quartz crystal

WHAT TO DO

1 Sit in a chair with your back straight but not rigid, using the chair back for support if necessary.

2 Relax your shoulders by stretching them up and down several times to release tension and stagnant *chi*. Shake out your hands vigorously for a minute to cleanse your emotions and stimulate the flow of *chi* to your hands.

3 Hold your large Clear Quartz crystal in front of you.

4 Take your starting exhalation. Breathe out through your nose by releasing all the air from your lungs as you would normally and then exhale completely by forcing the remaining air out of your lungs.

5 Then let your inhaling be the natural result of your exhaling, as you fill your lungs completely with air. Inhale very slowly through your nose, drawing your breath first into your abdomen to fill and expand it, then up through the middle of your body, finally expanding your chest by raising your breastbone.

6 On your next exhalation, contract your abdomen first as you breathe out, then your middle and chest by lowering your breastbone.

7 Focus on your Clear Quartz crystal, imagine you are breathing in its crystal energies and allow your eyes to close.

8 Be aware of your breathing and repeat this exercise seven times.

Fatigue

We all know what it is like to feel tired in the morning after a late night, or exhausted at the weekend after a hard week's work. This type of fatigue is a normal reaction to leading a busy life. It is when fatigue becomes persistent and chronic that it becomes a problem.

Fatigue may be a symptom of other emotional or physical problems from depression to diabetes. It is also common during the menopause, when women may be chronically deprived of sleep due to night sweats and insomnia.

Chronic fatigue syndrome (CFS) is a state of extreme physical and mental fatigue that disrupts normal life. As well as this abnormal tiredness, lack of energy, physical and mental weakness and lethargy, symptoms also include depression, joint pain, sleeping problems, sore throat, low-grade fever and an inability to perform ordinary daily tasks. CFS is also sometimes known as postviral syndrome (because the symptoms often first appear after a viral infection) or as ME (myalgic encephalomyelitis).

Seasonal affective disorder (SAD) is triggered by a lack of natural daylight, which can cause imbalanced brain chemical activity leading to fatigue, lethargy and poor concentration. It is sometimes referred to as the 'winter blues' as for many sufferers it is a cyclical problem that lessens when the long daylight hours of summer return.

Garden visualization crystals

- Citrine is stimulating and wakes you up. The crystals contain the energy of sunshine, optimism, warmth, joy, vitality, regeneration, clarity and focused mental awareness. Citrine restructures the mental body, and so stops energy drain, depletion and 'burn-out'. It is useful in relieving fatigue caused by illness or the menopause or even by other outside parasitic energies.

- Carnelian's signature is strong, stimulating and protective. It is used to repair the etheric body after shock, trauma, loss, illness or betrayal. It

ameliorates grief, including the grief associated with bereavement. It enhances creativity and optimism and induces a positive outlook on life. It eases fears and phobias by balancing the body's energy levels.

- Peridot dispels negative emotions. It brings youthful renewal, acting as a tonic to spring-clean the whole subtle-body system. Peridot banishes lethargy and fear of the unknown. It clears feelings of restriction, and so is especially useful for those who have been housebound or confined by illness.

Citrine

Carnelian

Peridot

Garden visualization

We all feel the need for a dynamic energy renewal at different times in our lives. Rejuvenation and renewal is part of the natural cycle of life. Our ancestors often took different combinations of herbs as a spring tonic. This visualization is a crystal healing tonic that promotes and supports energy renewal.

YOU WILL NEED

3 Citrine, tumbled

OR

3 Peridot, tumbled

OR

3 Carnelian, tumbled

NOTE You can use three crystals of the same kind or a mixture of all three. You may also substitute any other bright clear yellow, green or orange crystals of your choice.

WHAT TO DO

1 Lie down comfortably on the floor, using a yoga mat or pad if you prefer.

2 Place the three crystals so that they form a triangle around your body, with one above your head, and the other two out to the sides and just below your feet.

3 Relax your body by focussing on your breathing.

4 Visualize yourself in a garden. It could be a real place or somewhere that only exists in your imagination. It is your inner garden. Explore it. Are there plants and flowers growing there? Which ones? What size is this garden? Does it have fences, walls or other boundaries? What is beyond this garden? Is the sun shining or is it raining? What time of day is it? Try to engage all your senses in this visualization exercise. Can you feel the ground beneath your feet, or hear the wind rustling the trees or bird song? Can you smell the flowers?

5 This is your garden and it represents your energy, vitality and renewal. Remember, because it is your garden, everything is allowed. Is there anything in the garden you need to change or improve? Perhaps you need to plant a tree or flowers or remove some weeds? Does it need a water feature, perhaps a fountain or some other water source? Feel free to make any changes you wish.

6 Has anyone else access to your garden? If so, do you want them to be there with you?

7 Allow 15–30 minutes for this visualization and for your body to integrate the crystal energies.

Sleep disorders

Insomnia is difficulty in falling asleep, or in staying asleep, or in waking in the early hours of the morning and then not being able to get back to sleep. It may be acute or chronic. Acute insomnia is often caused by a significant traumatic life event such as bereavement. Chronic insomnia occurs when a spell of sleep disturbance becomes a pattern.

Before deciding that you have insomnia, become aware of your normal sleep pattern. Some people need eight hours of sleep a night, others only four or five, so don't try to sleep more than you need. Also be aware that sleep patterns can change, for example as we get older the need for one long period of sleep decreases to be replaced by more frequent shorter spells.

Stress is one of the main culprits when it comes to insomnia. To combat this, try a yoga-based relaxation technique or a period of meditation just before you go to bed. Alternatively, a simple breathing exercise can help enormously. Take a deep breath in through your nose, hold for the count of six and then exhale gently through your mouth while repeating the word 'peace' in your mind. Repeat ten times. You can also try placing an Amethyst under your pillow to aid peaceful sleep.

Nightmares can occur at any age and are often brought on by stress, anxiety or fear. Recurring nightmares are a sign that your subconscious mind is deeply troubled. Indigo-coloured crystals such as Iolite sedate the conscious mind bringing peaceful detachment from worldly concerns and so facilitate an internal dialogue with your deep subconscious. Placing an Iolite crystal under your pillow at night will give you insight into your nightmare situation.

Therapy tips

- Wind down properly before bedtime by creating a sleep ritual. Take a warm bath with a few drops of lavender essential oil added. Surrounding your bath with Amethyst crystals and lighting a few candles will aid relaxation and induce tranquillity. Try not to eat, read or watch TV in bed.

- Keep your bedroom warm, dark, quiet and well ventilated. Decorate it in soothing colours – all shades of violet and lavender induce relaxation and release stress. Place an Amethyst crystal at your bedside.

- Lavender is one of the herbs traditionally said to help insomnia. Place a bunch of dried lavender flowers on your bedside table or place a drop of lavender essential oil on your pillow.

- Avoid eating heavy meals or drinking stimulants such as coffee, tea and fizzy drinks after eight o'clock at night.

- Take regular exercise during the day, but do not exercise within two hours of going to bed.

- Only go to bed when you are sleepy. Try not to nap during the day or sleep in late during the morning.

Sweet dreams

Let your intuition help you choose the right stone for you for this crystal healing technique. If you feel that your insomnia is the result of stress, choose Amethyst. If you are a sensitive individual whose insomnia is caused by your fears, choose Sugilite. If your mind is troubled and you suffer from nightmares, choose Charoite or Iolite.

YOU WILL NEED

1 Amethyst, tumbled

OR

1 Sugilite, tumbled

OR

1 Charoite, tumbled

OR

1 Iolite, tumbled

WHAT TO DO

1 Lie down comfortably on your bed, preferably at bedtime.

2 Place the crystal you have chosen on your third eye chakra, in between your eyes at the top of your nose. This area is the main acupressure point for clearing the stagnant energy that may cause insomnia. Massaging the third eye chakra at bedtime also induces sleepiness.

3 You can leave the crystal in place while you fall asleep or remove it after 15 minutes and place it under your pillow.

Sweet dreams crystals

- Amethyst crystals purify the physical and subtle bodies, reaching deep into the body to clear the source of the insomnia. Amethyst also aids restful sleep by relieving tension and stress which are major causes of insomnia.

- Sugilite balances the nervous system. It brings relief to sensitive individuals who are prone to nightmares that are brought on by fear of people or situations.

- Charoite transforms fear into insight and eases emotional turmoil. It also helps infants sleep peacefully and will give protection from nightmares and insomnia.

- Iolite sedates the conscious mind by cleansing and activating the third eye chakra. It awakens inner knowing and wisdom.

PART 2

CRYSTALS TO BALANCE YOUR EMOTIONS

Crystals and your emotions

Our emotions are linked to the fluid element of water. Water has a special significance as most of our body weight is made up of water and it carries the nutrients essential for life.

One of the hardest aspects of balancing your emotions is actually identifying how you are feeling at any given time. Like water, emotions change constantly, ebbing and flowing, giving us movement that helps us explore our potential as humans. Sometimes emotions become frozen and we become stuck in a space that is restrictive and often destructive to our potential for happiness and creativity. Water when heated boils, then turns to steam and evaporates; this too can be reflected in the emotions of anger, loss and emptiness.

Ideally our emotions should be like a stream of fresh flowing water, constantly moving forwards. If a stream becomes blocked, it is no longer a stream, it becomes a stagnant muddy pool. Likewise our emotions must be fluid and life-affirming, bringing us exploration, joy and fulfilment. Too often people become bogged in emotions that trap them in a place of stagnation and restriction.

Crystals have the ability to transform stagnant energy by getting below the surface to the root of the problem. Emotional wounds lock up our energy, energy that we need to live life to the full. Crystals heal these wounds, restore our equilibrium and set our energy free.

Crystal healing uses some very effective techniques to release trauma without the need to go through the pain of reliving the event. They help the emotional body reintegrate the energy involved, an important part of healing. If instead we keep reliving the trauma, we become involved with intellectualizing it, causing ourselves even more stress and debilitation that may then bring on physical illness.

Watery crystals

- Moonstone and Selenite both have a natural affinity to the element of water. They are able to stabilize the emotions and balance body fluids.

- Aquamarine also relates to the watery element of the emotions, especially when a build-up of painful experiences has caused fear or phobias.

When the thymus gland becomes stressed because of emotional debilitation, it needs the energy boost that Aquamarine provides, which helps the body release the underlying cause of the dis-ease.

- Opal loves water. This stone is an emotional mirror that can stabilize mood swings.

Herkimer Diamond

Apophyllite

Diamond

Garnet

Colour and emotional healing

Your spontaneous response to colour is a great way of intuitively choosing a crystal to balance your emotions, as the different colours have different healing properties. Your choice of colour may also help you identify your underlying feelings.

CLEAR CRYSTALS

Clear crystals such as Clear Quartz, Danburite, Diamond, Phenacite, Azeztulite, Herkimer Diamonds or Apophyllite will throw light on your emotional situation. Just holding, carrying or wearing clear crystals will instantly lighten the emotions and bring peaceful harmony.

RED CRYSTALS

Red crystals help you to achieve your heart's desire. Ruby disperses imbalances of the heart such as guilt or unworthiness that may have blocked your self-confidence or courage. It also provides you with the emotional fuel to move forwards by releasing stagnation. Garnet and Zircon both lift melancholy

and will help you to find your inner strength and full potential, and release your fear of failure.

ORANGE CRYSTALS

Orange Carnelian heals the etheric body and so stops you withdrawing into a fantasy world. It can help to ground and focus your thoughts and emotions, protect you from hatred, envy and rage, and lift your spirits. If you suffer from existential fears, past physical abuse, vitality-sapping illness or any long-standing mental anguish, the negativity-banishing Carnelian is a good on-going life-force supplement.

Amber quickly heals gaps, holes, tears and other wounds in the aura caused by emotional imbalances. Wearing Amber gives protection against other people's negative emotions that may also cause auric damage.

PEACH CRYSTALS

Peach crystals such as Morganite, Peach Moonstone and Peach Calcite stabilize volatile emotions. They also help with self-love, especially for the parts of yourself you have judged and rejected as being unlovely, ugly or unlovable.

Ruby

Amber

Morganite

Yellow Sapphire

Emerald

Malachite

Peridot

YELLOW CRYSTALS

Yellow Citrine is energizing and uplifting, making it beneficial for those who suffer from depression. It also eases suicidal tendencies.

GREEN CRYSTALS

Green crystals such as Emerald, Dioptase, Malachite and Green Tourmaline are diagnostic, they get to the heart of the problem. Peridot heals the negative energy of the green ray – jealousy, resentment, selfishness, hypochondria, scarcity, hatred, greed and spite.

Pale Green Hiddenite releases the fear of failure. It is good for people who put on a brave face when their hearts are full of pain, helping them to honour these feelings and gently release them.

BLUE CRYSTALS

Lapis combats the mental cruelty, heals the martyr syndrome and aids emotional discrimination. Among other blue stones, Sodalite soothes the nervous system and Kyanite brings tranquillity.

Pale Blue Celestite, Angelite and Blue Lace Agate are expansive crystals. They bestow faith in yourself and instil in you the confidence to move forward by showing you new perspectives.

Turquoise and Chrysocolla help you express yourself, build your self-confidence, stimulate your creativity and balance the energies of your heart.

PURPLE CRYSTALS

Indigo Iolite helps those people who are undisciplined or distrustful, who may fear success and who may tend to set their sights too low.

Violet Charoite helps infants to sleep peacefully and will give protection from nightmares and insomnia. It releases hidden fears.

Amethyst, another violet crystal, is calming, soothing and stabilizing, quickly dispelling incoherent thought patterns and helping people who feel emotionally erratic.

PINK CRYSTALS

Pink crystals of Rose Quartz bring emotional healing. Pink Quartz is known as the love stone, it is a very seductive crystal that can be too dynamic for some people as it has the ability to transmute all stored-up

Sodalite

Blue Celestite

Violet Charoite

Rose Quartz

Kunzite

Morganite

Snow Quartz

putrefied negative issues of self-worth, self-confidence and self-acceptance. The very pale pink form is recommended as it is the most soothing. It will gently resolve any resistance you may have to releasing unresolved emotional stress.

Pale Pink Kunzite balances and integrates the head and heart energy centres. In our society there often seems to be war between the head and the heart, between science and the spirit of nature. If we are to understand the subtleties of emotional dis-ease we need to look at ourselves in a holistic way, and Kunzite will help.

Pink-Lavender is the colour found in some varieties of Smithsonite. These varieties have an energy that is soft, gentle, comforting and soothing. Many people subjugate or deny their true emotions and much emotional dis-ease stems from the repressed feelings of early childhood. The heavenly feel of Smithsonite heals the child within. It also works well on the brain's pain centres so it can help with alcohol- and drug-related emotional disorders.

Lepidolite with Rubellite supports self-esteem. It clears emotional negativity, fear and agression.

WHITE CRYSTALS

White stones such as Magnesite, Selenite, Milky Quartz or Snow Quartz can be very soothing to the emotions. They will cool down hot, inflamed or stressful feelings and situations.

BLACK CRYSTALS

Black stabilizing stones such Smoky Quartz and black grounding stones such as Haematite, Black Tourmaline and Jet bring emotional security. Magnetite can be used to alleviate negative emotional states by clearing energy blocks. Obsidian will go to the root cause of emotional imbalances and then release them. Onyx will release fears and worries as well as old emotional hurts that may have become buried deep within the subconscious.

MULTICOLOURED CRYSTALS

Gems that display several colours provide a spectrum of healing energies and are effective at bringing emotional balance. Opal amplifies personality traits, bringing them to the surface for healing. Abalone balances fear, anxiety and nervousness.

Haematite

Obsidian

Black Tourmaline

Depression

Depression can range from sadness to utter despair. No one can go through life without hitting some rough patches, times when we or a friend or family member suffer a loss or some serious disappointment that makes us feel sad, dejected, discouraged or despondent. We may also be more susceptible to illnesses, as depression also affects the immune system.

In the case of mild (situational) depression, the symptoms usually subside with time, rest and relaxation. However, people in the grip of major (clinical) depression that totally incapacitates them should seek professional help.

The symptoms of clinical depression vary with each individual but typically include at least five of the following, persisting for at least two weeks: feelings of hopelessness, helplessness, sadness, despair and worthlessness; loss of interest and pleasure in things; marked weight loss (when not dieting) and greatly decreased appetite; weight gain with compulsive eating; trouble falling or staying asleep, or sleeping more than normal; feeling jittery and restless or slow and lethargic; lack of motivation; fatigue and energy loss; trouble concentrating; thinking about or planning suicide.

Depression often runs in families, suggesting that your biological make-up may make you more likely to be depressed. There is no single definitive cause, but in certain at-risk individuals, a depressive reaction may be triggered by any highly stressful event or major life change, including bereavement, serious illness or accident, or emotional or physical abuse.

Common physical causes of depression include nutritional deficiencies, blood sugar imbalance, food intolerances, anaemia, long-term physical pain, thyroid problems and hormonal imbalances.

Hormonal changes around menstruation, after the birth of a baby or at the menopause may be causes of depression in women. Some people experience unexplained sadness, which can bring on periods of depression. Triggers for this type of depression are held in the subconscious mind and need releasing through therapy or counselling.

Positive affirmations can work wonders when it comes to banishing all kinds of negative emotional states, including depression. Many people spend a lot of time and energy looking at all the negative situations in their lives, how they hate their jobs, or don't want to smoke or be overweight. How many times a day do you recall a hurtful criticism or feel inferior or inadequate? By replacing these negative thoughts with positive thoughts (affirmations), you can change the way you feel about yourself.

Therapy tips

- A Clear Quartz pyramid or standing point is the best shape for broadcasting affirmations.

- Ideally leave the crystal and your affirmation in a position where they will be bathed in moonlight. The moon has a strong affinity with the subconscious mind.

- Working with the crystal kingdom is an excellent way of deprogramming yourself and clearing negative emotional states.

- Remember that you are what you believe!

Clear Quartz

Positive affirmations

Using affirmations conditions you to focus on what you really do want in life. Positive results can be obtained very quickly if affirmations are repeated as often as possible (that way the positive effect really registers and leaves less room for negative thinking). However, it would be difficult to spend hours every day repeating affirmations, and setting yourself such a task would be unrealistic. By using crystals to support the affirmation process you will speed up the release of subconscious limitations, self-doubt and negative emotional states.

YOU WILL NEED
1 Clear Quartz crystal

WHAT TO DO

1 Write out a positive affirmation for yourself. Make it as powerful and appropriate to you and your situation as possible. Use positive phrases ('I open my heart to healing all emotional discord'), not negative ('I don't want emotional discord in my life any more').

2 Cleanse and program your crystal using your chosen method (see page 13 for information on how to do this).

3 Place your affirmation under your crystal and leave them in a place where they will be undisturbed for as long as needed. Remember they are working for you 24 hours a day, seven days a week.

Bereavement

Bereavement touches all our lives. Coping with the loss of a loved one can be a difficult and stressful experience, often triggering depression. Losing a partner or close family member is a highly stressful life-changing event.

We may also suffer feelings of bereavement for our past, our lost youth, our missed opportunities. Some people fixate on past events, regrets or sorrows. Others want to bring their past into their present – it is as if they feel betrayed by the passage of time and wish to fix their entire life in a time capsule. They may regret growing older and try to pursue youth with expensive cosmetics and cosmetic procedures.

We should honour the past, but not dwell there to the detriment of our present. If you find that you start most of your sentences with the words 'I used to...' or 'When I was...', then you could be clinging to the past and have a lot of your life energy tied up there. Feelings of nostalgia, homesickness, remorse for having missed an opportunity, unfulfilled dreams or ambitions will also tie up your life energy. In the negative emotional state of permanent loss, the past can be overidealized, so weakening your connection with your current life situation.

One of the most important life principles is that of constant change, that everything is in a state of flux. We all need to be adaptable emotionally, and coping with changing circumstances needs us to live in the present moment. Living in the past depletes your life force and stops emotional growth.

Gem essence

This gem essence removes inertia and helps you bring your awareness into the present. It releases negative emotional states that make you overly glorify the past. It eases homesickness and remorsefulness over missed opportunities. Sunstone is very helpful in releasing the wistfulness for the so-called good old days that makes you expect nothing positive from the present.

YOU WILL NEED

1 Sunstone, tumbled or raw

WHAT TO DO

Make a gem essence (see page 14 for information on how to do this) and take it as directed.

Therapy tips

- Positive affirmations are very useful in removing negative emotional states, especially when combined with crystal therapy. Use the affirmation 'Every day is new, exciting and full of joy' when working with Sunstone.

- Carrying or wearing Sunstone will supplement the effect of the gem essence.

Sunstone

Shyness

Shy individuals often find the world a harsh place in which to live. Their trepidation is sometimes viewed as cowardice, although nothing could be further from the truth. They often have an endless list of fears, although they may try very hard to hide them. Their timidity and reserve can often make them appear aloof or arrogant.

In their heart of hearts, most shy people really do not want to have much to do with the normal world, feeling alienated by technology and preferring to withdraw and live in a fantasy realm. This withdrawal can make them vulnerable to phobias and depression. Failing to integrate into the world may also result in hypersensitivity to extremes of temperature, chemicals, noise, pollution, harsh words and conflict. Shy people habitually have cold hands and feet and blush easily, getting anxious or agitated when meeting new people or situations. They are often delicate physically, falling ill easily and recovering slowly, requiring a protracted convalescent period.

Shyness is the sign of a sensitive soul. Those who are sensitives need to understand that their shyness and sensitivity are not diseases to be conquered but refinements of the soul. Unfortunately, they are often unsure of themselves and their own unique abilities, so they can be easily intimidated by others. Shy, timid people are peaceful and very rarely show signs of anger or rage, knowing that any loss of temper always makes them feel drained of energy and emotionally disempowered. They need to create their own sacred space where they can recuperate.

Meditation comes easily to sensitive souls who, once supportive measures have been put in place, have the potential to make wonderful healers and clairvoyants. In fact they often excel in all the arts, making excellent musicians, actors, writers, poets and painters. Once those who are shy and sensitive understand that they have a precious gift and learn to develop their abilities, they instantly release their fears, phobias and inhibitions.

Gem essence

This supportive essence has been found very helpful by gentle sensitive souls who find it difficult to screen out the negativity and hostility of others. It can provide feelings of security and protection amid the harsh climate of the negative earth vibrations of hostility, rage, anger and fear, and help to integrate the spiritual body with the physical body.

YOU WILL NEED
1 Sugilite, tumbled

WHAT TO DO
Make a gem essence (see page 14 for information on how to do this) and take it as directed.

Sugilite

Shock

Everyone at some point in their life will encounter shocking experiences that leave them unable to cope. These acute moments of crisis may be exceptional circumstances such as accidents, a sudden illness, the sudden death of a loved one, even natural or man-made disasters. But physical experiences are not the only cause of shock, it can also be emotional or spiritual in origin.

Shock initially causes vulnerability in the solar plexus chakra as the stimulus overload causes it to freeze in the wide-open position. This subtle-energy breakdown or 'energetic trauma' can be sensed by the sufferer, who may feel as if they have received a physical blow to the solar plexus. It can also be seen by those who are clairvoyant. Untreated it deeply stresses the chakras above and below the solar plexus, causing each of them to go out of alignment.

The etheric body (aura) is ripped asunder, often torn into shreds (in severe life-threatening situations the aura turns grey and disintegrates). The nervous system is unable to cope, causing all chakra centres to fall out of alignment. A person in shock is thus unable to tune into their higher self (the superconscious mind) and feels disconnected from reality. In severe cases, shock causes subtle-body breakdown causing physical body rigidity — feeling and being petrified.

Energetic trauma brings on a multitude of emotions from bemusement, grief and mental numbness to feeling as though the whole world is falling apart. Trauma left untreated may develop into phobias and post-traumatic stress disorder (PTSD).

Sensitive people and children who do not yet have a fully developed subtle-energy system will be shocked by outside influences more easily than an adult with a well-developed energetic system. Each shock and resulting trauma depletes our life-force, often registered first by the kidneys through overactive adrenal glands. Those who have experienced traumatic births or childhoods find they can quickly deplete their energy reserves in adult life.

Restoring equilibrium crystals

- Carnelian releases trauma, heals the aura and balances the sacral chakra.

- Rutile Quartz restores the natural movement of life energy by repairing damaged structures on all levels. It also reorganizes energy integrity.

- Turquoise crystals release stress by relaxing the shoulders and upper body.

- Rose Quartz is revitalizing, heals emotions, releases stress and stimulates healing. It maintain energy levels by providing protection against those unwanted influences from the outside world that many sensitive souls find overwhelming.

Carnelian

Rutile Quartz

Turquoise

Rose quartz

Restoring equilibrium

Energetic trauma should ideally be released quickly, as delay may leave you vulnerable to outside influences that you may perceive as dark and threatening. This will not always be possible, as although most shock impacts immediately, the resulting trauma may not fully appear for weeks or months. This healing technique can be used to recall and release past shock, including traumatic births and childhoods.

YOU WILL NEED

7 Rutile Quartz, tumbled

3 Carnelian, tumbled

3 Rose Quartz, tumbled

1 Turquoise, tumbled

WHAT TO DO

1 Lie down comfortably on the floor, using a yoga mat or pad if you prefer.

2 Place six Rutile Quartz around your body, one above your head, one beneath your feet and two at each side of the body, at the knees and the elbows. Place the final one on your solar plexus.

3 Place one Carnelian at your throat chakra, one on your sacral chakra and one between your knees (see page 18 for the locations of the chakras).

4 Place one Rose Quartz on your heart chakra and the other two on the stress-release points at the temples.

5 Place the Turquoise over your thymus (between the throat and heart chakras, where your collarbones meet).

6 Allow yourself to recall the traumatic event. This facilitates release and the subsequent repair process. When you feel a change of emotion and a return of equilibrium the process will be complete.

7 Repeat the technique until your intuition tells you that equilibrium is fully restored.

Pessimism

People who suffer from habitual pessimism distrust not only themselves and their own abilities but the world and everyone and everything in it. They do not seem to understand that doubt attracts negative outcomes. The universe always gives you exactly what you expect. The expression 'I will believe it when I see it' could be turned around to 'You will see it when you believe it'.

These melancholy souls overanalyze everything. They have a rigid 'mental body' that constrains them into scrutinizing, pondering and contemplating everything in such minute detail that all joy and spontaneity is sucked out of every situation. They actually enjoy establishing just how badly things are going for them and gain deep satisfaction when they are proved right. Delighting in the company of other pessimists, they only feel truly comfortable in the company of others who, like them, are full of fear.

Yellow Calcite medicine

- Yellow Calcite cleanses the mental body of the blockages that cause pessimism. It quickly restores our gratitude and joy for life. This allows the flow of healthy balanced scepticism while removing the negativity of pessimism.

Yellow Calcite

Gem essence

Everyone can be subject to the odd bout of pessimism, those moments of self-doubt that usually occur when life is beset by obstacles. These temporary blockages in the mental body can be released through crystal healing. If you are normally optimistic but are experiencing minor setbacks, try combining this gem essence with the positive affirmation 'I am grateful for all the joy and happiness that flows into my life'.

YOU WILL NEED
1 Yellow Calcite, tumbled

NOTE: You can use a Citrine crystal if you do not have Yellow Calcite.

WHAT TO DO
Make a gem essence (see page 14 for information on how to do this) and take it as directed.

Hopelessness

Hopelessness occurs when normal positive mental programming becomes entrenched in negativity, an apathetic resignation that stops feelings of joy from flowing. Feeling desperate and unhappy with your situation, you are unable to lift your spirits and see the light at the end of what seems to be a long dark tunnel. Hopelessness is an energetic capitulation into thinking that you have a life sentence of unhappiness ahead of you and nothing can be done to change your fate.

Hopelessness is a personality trait that may be learnt in our early childhood if our essential needs for warmth, nourishment and protection are not met. Babies who are left to cry for hours when they are hungry will come to realize that their needs are never met and it is hopeless for them to have expectations to the contrary. These feelings may then persist into adult life, causing restriction.

Brazilianite medicine

- Brazilianite increases life-force, so bringing protection to the subtle-energy systems of the body. It releases limitations by easing bitterness regarding past relationships, and helps you to cope with loneliness, overcome hopelessness and find contentment. Physically, Brazilianite revitalizes the nervous and digestive systems. Emotionally and intellectually, it awakens ambitions that bring spontaneity combined with joy.

Brazilianite

Gem essence

Energetically the solar plexus chakra links to our mental body and nervous system. It controls how we view the world and is our most powerful tool for creating the belief systems that can change our personal circumstances. When the solar plexus chakra becomes distorted or damaged, instead of being in its normal position pointing outwards (and slightly upwards in the case of optimists), it points downwards, resembling a wilted dying flower. Brazilianite opens, clarifies, regenerates and balances the solar plexus chakra, restoring its flower to life and so in turn lifting your spirits.

YOU WILL NEED
1 Brazilianite, natural, with single termination, or raw

WHAT TO DO
Make a gem essence (see page 14 for information on how to do this) and take it as directed.

Apathy

Paralyzing apathy occurs when all emotions and sensations have disappeared, rendering us completely passive to all outside situations and stimuli (apathy literally means 'without feeling'). This is stagnation at the level of the soul, where we become fatalistically resigned to everything. This severe condition is due to the crown chakra being damaged, causing detachment from the higher self (the superconscious mind).

Our crown chakra links us to our uplifting, universal source of energy and information. When it is closed or trapped in an inappropriately low level of activity, it stops the flow of energy to all the lower chakras. This type of damage may be caused by chronic disease or severe illness that has not responded well to conventional treatment, or in any other circumstances where closing yourself down completely seems less frightening than the alternatives.

The lesser traits of lethargy, disinterest, boredom and indifference are often due to overwhelming sadness caused by external circumstances that have caused us to give up hope. In these cases it is the solar plexus chakra (which rules the mental body) that has become distorted or damaged.

Gem essence

In all cases of apathy, lethargy, indifference and boredom the solar plexus and the crown chakras both need to be repaired, balanced and integrated. This gem essence emphasises the positive, and creating a positive affirmation for yourself (see page 77 for information on how to do this) will reinforce the healing qualities of this crystal healing technique. You could also carry or wear some or all of the crystals used in this gem essence to further speed up the healing process. Creating a positive affirmation to reinforce this technique speeds up the process even more.

YOU WILL NEED

1 Amblygonite, natural

1 Apophyllite, natural

1 Heliodor, natural or tumbled

1 Herkimer Diamond, natural, with double termination

1 Phenacite, natural

1 Yellow Sapphire, natural or tumbled

NOTE If you do not have access to all these crystals use a combination of as many of them as possible.

WHAT TO DO

Make a combined gem essence (see page 14 for information on how to do this) and take it as directed.

Positivity crystals

- Amblygonite is pale lemon in colour. It is energetically soothing and inspiring to the mental body, giving a flowing graceful energy of calm and peace. It provides divine inspiration. Amblygonite will, with conscious direction, clear damage to the etheric body and can be used to activate any chakra, especially the higher centres above the head. It brings the consciousness of the higher self into the spiritual body.

- Apophyllite connects the physical body with the etheric realms and will expand your awareness of subtle-energy, which clears blockages and stagnation in the higher chakra centres. This clear crystal releases anxiety and worries from the emotional body and releases negative thought patterns from the mental body.

- Heliodor (Golden Beryl) heals stress in the mental body by activating and integrating the crown and solar plexus chakras. It opens gateways to our understanding of the archetypal realms. By giving you a greater understanding of the role you are playing in your life drama, it allows you to step out of the illusion to view your true situation more clearly. This promotes greater mental and emotional stability.

- Herkimer Diamonds contain a brilliant clear light energy that facilitates a balanced dynamic flow of information between the chakra centres.

- Phenacite has a very high vibration that cleanses, activates and aligns all the chakras. It is especially beneficial to the higher chakra centres, bringing an enhanced state of awareness. This enhanced state reinforces the universal law of resonance – like attracts like – and so by focussing day after day on the positive it becomes deeply imbedded in your neural pathways.

- Yellow Sapphire is expansive to the mental body and increases understanding and intelligence. It attracts positive energy which facilitates a beneficial outcome.

Amblygonite

Apophyllite

Yellow Sapphire

Phenacite

Herkimer Diamond

Helidor

Abandonment

When we feel disconnected from our sources of hope, happiness and inspiration, we frequently feel abandoned. This causes us to stop making any efforts towards making positive life changes. We become resigned to our fate, passively surrendering to the negative life situations in which we find ourselves. Lethargy sets in as we lose all motivation to change our unhappy circumstances. It does not matter what initially caused your feelings of being abandoned, whether it was an unhappy home life, an unsatisfactory job, chronic illness or financial problems. At some point you became demotivated and negative programming became deeply entrenched and anchored into your mental body.

When the mental body becomes distorted by negative anchors, the solar plexus chakra closes down, only allowing a small amount of life energy to enter. The chakras above and below also become starved of life-force.

To restore energetic balance, an influx of positive energy is required from an outside stable force. This is where gemstones with their stable molecular 'signature' are very useful tools of self-transformation. If we administer positive energy, which vibrates at a higher frequency, then the body simply raises its vibration. The negative anchors attached to the mental body are released and the body quickly assumes its normal frequency.

Gem essence

Fire Opal is an excellent crystal for those who feel disconnected, abandoned, chronically bored, washed out, indifferent and empty. Try this gem essence if you always feel tired with no energy and are apathetically vegetating, are feeling completely abandoned by the universe or if you are resigned to your fate and passively surrendering to the negative life situation in which you find yourself.

YOU WILL NEED
1 Fire Opal, natural

WHAT TO DO
Make a gem essence (see page 14 for information on how to do this) and take it as directed.

Fire Opal

Loneliness

People who experience feelings of loneliness or isolation sometimes find that their problems really started in early childhood when they suffered emotional deprivation. They did not receive the necessary affection and appreciation they required to allow them to grow into balanced individuals. When children are denied emotional support and nourishment, they may grow into adults who will often express feelings of being lonely. Even when they are surrounded by other people, they will still feel alone or isolated.

The opposite condition also arises from early emotional deprivation. It surfaces as self-centredness, self-obsession, being emotionally demanding or a talkative hypochondriac. These people cannot bear to be alone, they must be the centre of attention. They feed off the emotional energies of others and sap their strength with their incessant talking, which is always about themselves. These self-absorbed, self-centred, demanding individuals are always poor listeners who tend to exaggerate emotionally, making mountains out of molehills.

Loneliness and self-centredness, extrovert personality or introvert, both stem from childhood emotional deprivation. Both relate to a heart chakra that is out of balance and distorted. Both show a lack of empathy with others and a need to embrace the world and reach out to others with love.

Gem essence

The crystals used in this gem essence are the pink and green forms of the mineral Spodumene. Both bring wholeness and balance to the emotional body. Kunzite awakens unconditional love for the self and others within the heart centre. It supports newborns and children by helping them integrate within the Earth vibration. Hiddenite brings in the pale green ray of tender, gentle heart healing. It sensitively dispels negative emotions and feelings by releasing the old heartache of emotional depravation. Together they allow empathy with others to be established.

YOU WILL NEED
1 Kunzite, natural
1 Hiddenite, natural

WHAT TO DO
Make a combined gem essence (see page 14 for information on how to do this) and take it as directed.

Kunzite　　　　**Hiddenite**

Abuse

Abuse must never be tolerated, whether it be sexual, physical, emotional, mental or spiritual abuse. If you are being or have been abused, you need to seek expert help and support. In some people the effects of abuse will be immediate and obvious, in others they may not appear until years later, long after the abuse has stopped. They can range from bruises to antisocial behaviour to sexual promiscuity to total emotional withdrawal.

Abusive relationships (especially where domestic violence is involved) are frequently linked to substance abuse by the abuser, the victim or both. It is a mistake, however, to think that drug or alcohol dependency causes the abusive behaviour. It merely gives abusers excuses to hide behind, allowing them to evade responsibility for their actions. Healthcare professionals understand the only course of action is to examine the underlying cause of both the violent behaviour and the substance abuse and to treat both problems. Abusive relationships are toxic to all parties involved and need to be healed as soon as possible.

Serenity crystals

- Green Jade brings serenity when it is worn, carried or used as a gem essence. It instils wisdom, promotes feelings of tranquillity, cleanses feelings of self-disgust and stabilizes the personality. This stone harmonizes relationships on all levels and heals nervous stress caused by outside influences.

- Danburite is seen as a cure-all because of its ability to modify any condition. It clears karmic debris and links you to serenity and wisdom from the angelic realms.

- Aquamarine gives freedom from the impressions and influences of others. It releases the underlying patterns of dis-ease, instils courage and fortitude, and removes the victim mentality.

- Morganite cleanses stress and unexpressed feelings from the heart chakra. It holds the emotional body stable while deep healing takes place. It clears both conscious and unconscious negative programming.

Gem essence

This gem essence is created from crystals that should all help to bring serenity into your life. It will reinforce the support and advice you have been given by healthcare and other professionals.

YOU WILL NEED
1 Green Jade, tumbled

1 Danburite, tumbled

1 Aquamarine, tumbled

1 Morganite, tumbled

WHAT TO DO
Make a combined gem essence (see page 14 for information on how to do this) and take it as directed.

Lovelessness

Some people are so introverted that they feel totally bereft and loveless. These unfortunate souls never expect anything but failure, they are hesitant and passive, they lack any self-confidence. Their self-esteem is so low that they apologize for everything, even when they have no need to. They automatically feel inferior to everyone else.

The feelings of being useless, impotent and loveless usually start in infancy when the child takes on and absorbs the negative attitudes of their parents. This parental negative-programming causes severe distortion and malfunction of the solar plexus chakra, which adversely affects the mental body, preventing you from achieving heart-felt goals in life.

Mental body cleansing

Used daily, this crystal healing technique will dissolve the self-limiting concepts in your personality and allow the true potential of your soul to come to fruition. It can be used for long-term therapy and also for dealing with temporary problems relating to self-confidence. It is very useful before any activity or situation where you need a healthy boost of positive energy and self-esteem.

YOU WILL NEED

1 Clear Quartz, with single termination

WHAT TO DO

1 Cleanse your hands by holding them under cold running water, then drying them.

2 Cleanse your emotions by shaking out your hands for 2 minutes. This releases blocked energy in the heart chakra.

3 Begin to sensitize and raise the *chi* in your hands by rolling the Clear Quartz crystal between your palms for 2–5 minutes. Put the crystal down.

4 Slowly bring your palms together, feel the energy tingling between your hands, begin to feel the pressure as your hands come closer together. Play with this energy, bouncing it between your hands.

5 Form this energy into a sphere, visualize it as yellow in colour. When your intuition tells you it feels right, place this ball of energy into your solar plexus centre. This will energize, heal and balance your mental body.

Clear Quartz

Uncertainty

Uncertainty can cause mood swings, where you swing from one extreme of emotion to the other. One day you are enthusiastic and full of life over a new idea or project, then the next day you are miserable and apathetic and wonder what got into you. This constant vacillation makes knowing you unpleasant and uncomfortable for your family and friends. It is not much fun for you either as you flip-flop aimlessly between moods and opinions.

Your frequent mood swings and uncertainty cause you constant bewilderment. Your indecision causes inner restlessness, which often ends up as indifferent total exhaustion. You may have suffered from this condition all your life, as it probably relates to birth trauma or to a chaotic environment soon after birth where you were exposed to too many impressions, all bombarding you at once. Uncertainty can also lead to anxiety and panic attacks.

Inner balance crystals

- Clear Quartz is the master healer because of its broad spectrum of healing energies (see page 12). Smoky Quartz gives grounding and stability that stops extreme fluctuation of moods. Used together, with the Clear Quartz above your head and the Smoky Quartz beneath your feet, they release feelings of unease. They work together to realign your body along the central governing meridian and master chakra lines.

- Iolite strengthens your intuition, which aids inner balance and being centred. It improves powers of concentration and determination regardless of outside influences or circumstances. Iolite makes you more receptive to information and communication with your higher self.

- Rose Quartz revitalizes, heals emotions, releases stress and stimulates healing. It maintain energy levels by giving protection against those unwanted influences from the outside world that many impressionable souls find overwhelming. This crystal helps you develop empathy with your higher self, so increasing positive inner guidance.

- Moonstone nurtures the soul and heals the subtle-energy system by comforting and aiding serene contemplation. An excellent stone to hold in meditation, it releases emotional tension (especially trauma caused during or soon after birth), brings equilibrium and stops nervous tension, erratic behaviour and indecisiveness.

Smoky Quartz

Iolite

Clear Quartz

Moonstone

Rose Quartz

YOU WILL NEED

1 Clear Quartz, with single termination

1 Smoky Quartz, with single termination

1 Iolite, tumbled

3 Rose Quartz, tumbled

3 Moonstone, tumbled

WHAT TO DO

1 Lie down comfortably on the floor, using a yoga mat or pad if you prefer.

2 Place the Clear Quartz above your head and the Smoky Quartz beneath your feet, both with their terminations facing away from your body.

3 Place the Iolite on your third eye chakra (see page 18 for the location of the chakras).

4 Place one Rose Quartz on your heart chakra and one at the top of each of your shoulders.

5 Place the Moonstone crystals on your throat, solar plexus and sacral chakras.

6 Relax your body by focussing on your breathing. As you breathe out, focus on the word 'relax', and as you breathe in, focus on the word 'balance'.

7 Allow 20 minutes for your body to integrate the energies. Be ready to remove the crystals sooner if your intuition tells that you have integrated the crystal energy more quickly.

Inner balance

Because your opinions and moods change from one moment to the next, You will need to do everything in your power to reach your own inner centre, your own natural balance. The alternative is to spend your life falling under the influence of many passing forces. Use this powerful crystal healing technique to strengthen your intuition and end the dualistic erratic polarity shifts that make your life miserable.

Anxiety

Anxiety caused by stress can lead to physical problems such as high blood pressure, as well as to emotional concerns such as uneasiness, panic attacks, sleep disorders and nightmares. Everyday situations often cause stress. A visit to the dentist, an exam, a driving test, a job interview or a difficult neighbour or work colleague can often leave you feeling stressed and anxious.

When you experience anxiety, your body no longer functions with a balanced flow of energy. If you cannot release this anxiety, you can become ill or lose the ability to cope with your worries.

Amethyst

Therapy tips

- Make sure that you allow your body time to integrate the new flow of energy. Some people integrate the energy of Amethyst crystals very quickly, others may need several days or weeks for the healing process to take its natural course.

- After healing with Amethyst crystals, give yourself plenty of time to return to everyday awareness and normal breathing. Drink plenty of water to flush out any toxins that may have been released during the therapy session.

- Sometimes your witness point may feel tender or tingling for several hours. This effect is normal and will soon pass.

Clearing anxiety

Amethyst crystals heal the emotions, but they also reach deep into the body to heal the source of anxiety, even at the cellular level. They can help to clear distress from your physical body, soothe panic, aid restful sleep and ease nightmares. This simple technique is an effective and safe procedure, even for a beginner in crystal healing. It can be used on yourself and on others, as many times as needed.

YOU WILL NEED
1 Amethyst, with single termination

WHAT TO DO

1. Prepare and cleanse your Amethyst (see page 13 for information on how to do this).

2. Sit comfortably on the floor with your legs crossed. Place the crystal at your left side.

3. Place your hands in your lap, with the right hand resting on the left hand. Pull your shoulders back slightly to ease the blood flow to the brain.

4. Allow your eyes to close. Begin with 5 minutes of deep breathing to bring oxygen to your brain. Then slow your breathing and turn your full attention to the movement of your breath. Do not try to control your breathing; simply be aware of the breath entering and leaving your body.

5 With your right hand, tap your witness point three times. The witness point is located on your breastbone between your heart and your throat. Return your right hand to your lap and become aware of your witness point. You may feel a tingling or throbbing sensation as it begins to activate.

6 Pick up the Amethyst, hold it in your left hand with the termination pointing towards your head, and gently hold the crystal to your witness point. Think about the stressful situation you have chosen to release. Feel all the emotions associated with the anxiety and bring the full memory into your conscious awareness. Allow the distress to well up in your body.

7 Suddenly you will feel all the anxiety draining away. Your emotions will quickly become calm and focused.

8 Keep holding the Amethyst at your witness point. Often you will feel another surge of energy as the crystalline energy goes deeper. This surging feeling may occur several times as your body absorbs the healing energy of the Amethyst. Each time you feel the surge, be aware that your body has chosen to heal at a deeper level.

9 Cleanse your crystal after use.

Trauma

Any sudden frightening or shocking experience, be it physical, emotional, mental or spiritual, may result in energetic trauma if it cannot be immediately released by the energy system. This energetic trauma is then stored in both the physical body and the subtle-energy body.

Trauma is defined as any direct energy impact that our energetic system is unable to cope with. It can embed itself deep within the energy system, causing distortion in the overall energy flow and function. Some shocks will show immediate physical affects, others live on in the energetic system causing a degree of paralysis in the area under its influence. The sacral chakra stores and directs the overall flow of life energy, so this is where the first impact of trauma is often felt.

Trauma can influence us on many levels, even subconsciously, causing fear, apprehension, dread or nightmares. The aura can be torn or ripped by traumatic experiences and these tears can result in severe energy depletion. Trauma affects the way we feel and think, and locks up our energy in the distortion. This causes our energy system to come under stress, which again leads to energy depletion and chronic ill health.

Gem essence

We should always be aware that everything is energy, vibrating at different frequencies. Your health and wellbeing need your energy frequency to be balanced. This combined gem essence of Carnelian and Rutile Quartz will cause a rapid release of not only the initial trauma but the resulting stress the distortion caused in your energy systems. The Carnelian heals your auric wounds and balances your sacral chakra, while the Rutile Quartz restores the natural movement of life energy by repairing damaged structures on all levels.

YOU WILL NEED
1 Carnelian, tumbled
1 Rutile Quartz, tumbled

WHAT TO DO
Make a combined gem essence (see page 14 for information on how to do this) and take it as directed.

Rutile Quartz

Carnelian

Frustration

The angry emotion that is frustration is caused by a lack of patience that makes everyone else seem inadequate or a failure. People who frequently feel frustrated often have minds that work very quickly. Because they are quick-thinking, everyone else seems very slow to them.

On a physical level, frustration leads to inner tension, nervous exhaustion, nervous indigestion, hot flushes and skin irritation or rashes. Frustrated people may also be more accident prone and reckless.

Emotionally it can leads you to believe that you are superior to others and to forget your own shortcomings or failures. It is important for those who suffer from frustration to realize that they are no more important than anyone else.

Mentally it brings rigid attitudes, especially towards competitiveness and the acquisition of wealth. The mental body relates to the solar plexus chakra, and frustration causes the solar plexus to become distorted by too much energy. This can lead to a craving for power over everyone else.

Spiritually frustration entices us to believe we are so superior to others that we forget to listen to the wisdom they have to offer. This includes ignoring the guidance of not only the higher self but also of our angels and spirit guides.

Gem essence

Heliodor (also called Golden Beryl) brings mental and emotional stability by activating and integrating your crown chakra with your solar plexus chakra. This heals the impatient attitudes that cause frustration, stress and distortion in your mental body. By expanding your crown chakra to bring in higher guidance, it allows your solar plexus chakra to shine with the clarity of the sun. This expanded awareness allows you to view the broader perspective where false judgments about yourself and others can be released.

YOU WILL NEED

1 Heliodor, natural or tumbled

WHAT TO DO

Make a gem essence (see page 14 for information on how to do this) and take it as directed.

Helidor

Guilt

Guilt can affect your whole life and destroy the joy in your soul. If we try to understand where this guilt originates, we frequently find the seeds were sown in early childhood. Guilt-ridden people often turn out to have been the scapegoat of the family, or they were simply unwanted. Made to feel that they were at fault simply for having been born, unloved and never good enough, they strove to please their parents, always without success.

Those who are guilt-ridden are never really satisfied with themselves. They are perfectionists who despite many positive experiences blame themselves for not taking more trouble in everything they do.

The person who is obsessed by guilt will use apologetic turns of phrase in every conversation, such as 'I'll never forgive myself' or 'I know it was all my fault'. Their self-reproach and self-blame is limitless. They regret everything and forgive themselves nothing. They even take the blame for other's mistakes, as their masochistic desire to sacrifice themselves knows no limits.

Their guilt feelings can often cut them off from loving relationships or draw them into unsuitable relationships with inconsiderate partners. Anyone who holds on to guilt, unable to love and forgive themselves, is also unable to love and forgive others.

Halite and sea salt medicine

- Halite, a form of sodium chloride, is also known as rock salt. It is available in several colours – white, blue, lavender, purple, pink, green, yellow, brown or colourless – depending on where it comes from in the world.

- Blue Halite purifies the etheric body of past negative communication and ideologies. It gives self-recognition allowing you to understand your sin has already been forgiven. Every human being deserves loving relationships, and Blue Halite allows you to love yourself just as you are. It is helpful in establishing realistic goals.

- Pink Halite is especially useful in purifying the heart centre of past negative emotional programming that has been instilled during childhood. It removes deep-seated unconscious

concepts of good and evil, which frequently have a religious connotation. It releases the notion of original sin and of sex being sinful.

- Sea salt (also a form of sodium chloride) draws out negative energies from not only the physical body, but from all the subtle bodies as well. Olive oil renews life-force and restores harmony and balance.

Halite

Purification and rejuvenation

Feelings of guilt will affect your energy levels. If you are constantly tired and suffer from low energy, you need to renew your life-force. This simple crystal healing technique can be used often to cleanse the energy of guilt and remove the need for self-punishment. Halite baths and salt rubs have both proved useful in removing deep-seated negative emotional programming.

YOU WILL NEED

1 Halite, natural

Olive oil

Sea salt

NOTE: Choose blue or pink halite for this technique.

WHAT TO DO

1 Take a cleansing bath. Run a bath of comfortably warm water, place the Halite crystal into the bath, climb in, lean back and relax. Your guilt will simply dissolve away, just like the Halite crystal.

2 Follow your bath with a salt rub. Mix a teaspoon of olive oil and a teaspoon of sea salt together in the palm of your hand. Rub yourself all over using small circular movements, always working towards your heart. Rinse off in the shower and pat yourself dry.

Therapy tips

- If you want your Halite crystal to last for several baths, remove it after a small portion has dissolved.

- You can add two drops of essential oil to your bath. Pine is especially good as it cleanses feelings of guilt and self-blame, lavender is relaxing, and rose imbues the energy of love, both for the self and for others. You could also add a handful of fragrant herbs or flower petals to your bath water.

- You can also add two drops of pine, lavender or rose essential oil to the salt rub mixture.

Worry

Sometimes we have emotional issues or memories we can't resolve. We don't want to think about them, but the unwanted thoughts constantly come to mind and can't be turned off. We keep worrying about them, going over them time and time again until they become an obsession that is supercharged with mental energy.

Worry becomes mental hyperactivity, causing severe distortion to the mental body. It is as if our thoughts are caught in an endless loop. We may have trouble sleeping, especially in the early hours of the morning, then we are tired and depressed during the day. If we cannot silence this internal dialogue of tormented thoughts and mental arguments, we develop mental tension and chronic headaches.

Dispersing worry crystals

- Kunzite clears emotional energy that has become stuck in the obsessive loop of worry.

- Lepidolite desensitizes the nervous system and clears emotional debris that has distorted the mental body. It releases stress, worry and nervous tension. This crystal clears spaces of emotional or mental tension, especially after arguments or other highly charged emotional encounters.

Kunzite

Lepidolite

Dispersing worry

This crystal web breaks the endless cycle of worry by discharging the mental and emotional energy that has become stuck and prevented resolution of the underlying problem. You can support this particular technique by wearing a Rose Quartz or Amethyst pendant for additional stress relief.

YOU WILL NEED
2 Kunzite, natural
5 Lepidolite, tumbled

WHAT TO DO

1 Lie down comfortably on the floor, using a yoga mat or pad if you prefer.

2 Place one Kunzite above your head and one Kunzite beneath and between your feet.

3 Place the Lepidolite crystals on your third eye, throat, heart, solar plexus and sacral chakras (see page 18 for their locations).

4 Allow 20 minutes for your body to integrate the energies. Be ready to remove the crystals sooner if your intuition tells that you have integrated the crystal energy more quickly.

Exhaustion

Exhaustion happens when you spend a long time under a great deal of strain and your psyche does not have time to rejuvenate itself. You may have been ill, been overworked, not had enough sleep or been spending all your time and energy caring for someone else. A poor diet can also contribute to exhaustion, because your body then lacks the nutrients it needs for rejuvenation.

Severe exhaustion occurs when you are physically, emotionally, mentally and spiritually burned out and constantly drained of energy. Even the smallest task becomes an insurmountable obstacle. People who quite frequently find themselves in this state are often overconscientious and have not learned to channel their energies correctly by harmonizing the many different levels within their psyche.

Citrine medicine

- Citrine contains the energy of sunshine, it is stimulating, wakes you up and brings focused mental awareness. This crystal is full of optimism, warmth, joy, vitality, regeneration and clarity.

- Citrine revives and uplifts the solar plexus chakra. It restructures the mental body and stops energy drain, depletion and burn-out. This crystal relieves exhaustion and fatigue caused by illness, overwork, sleep deprivation or any activity that has led you to deplete your energy reserves. It can also re-energize you if you have been energetically drained by outside parasitic energies.

Gem essence

Crystal healing with Citrine is very effective at revitalizing and stabilizing the solar plexus chakra. This chakra is the main centre of rejuvenation, because it interfaces with many of the body's systems, including the nervous system, immune system, digestive system, the brain and the memory. It is also the centre of personal power and emotional stability. You can support the work of this gem essence by carrying or wearing a Citrine at all times, or by placing a Citrine crystal on a photograph of yourself (this also works for friends or family members who need a boost of positive energy).

YOU WILL NEED
1 Citrine, natural, with single termination, or tumbled

WHAT TO DO
Make a gem essence (see page 14 for information on how to do this) and take it as directed.

Citrine

Feeling overwhelmed

Sometimes you can feel overwhelmed by circumstances, despondent, as if a dark cloud has descended, covering you like a cloak of melancholia. The energy of deep gloom descends and overwhelms you for no apparent reason. It robs you of your soul qualities of cheerfulness and inner serenity, and can lead to complete energy depletion, black depression and breakdown. Many people find this dark energy leaves them feeling utterly disjointed, almost as if they are strangers in their lives.

We do not have to be weak-willed or inadequate to attract this energy into our life. Sensitive people often pick up emotional debris from others or from the environment. Negative thoughts then intrude and influence every aspect of life. This prevents us from reaching goals, dreams and ambitions.

Therapy tips

- Use more Clear Quartz or Labradorite crystals if you wish to make your circle larger. You can also include white candles in your circle of light.

- Remember to cleanse all the crystals thoroughly before and especially after use (see page 13 for information on how to do this).

- Wearing or carrying a Labradorite or Kunzite crystal will protect your heart energy integrity, allowing you to stay in the flow of universal love and compassion.

Clear Quartz

Labradorite

Kunzite

Circle of light

Some people describe the feeling of being overwhelmed as having an outside, unknown, negative energy that is overshadowing them and separating them from their soul. This crystal healing technique is excellent for releasing these dark energies. It can be used whenever you need to clear unwanted energy or place a protective circle of light around yourself and your home.

YOU WILL NEED

6 Labradorite, tumbled
6 Clear Quartz, with single terminations
1 Kunzite, natural

WHAT TO DO

1 Place the Labradorite and Clear Quartz alternately in a circle around you. Sit cross-legged in the centre of the circle.

2 Hold the Kunzite to your heart chakra (see page 18) using both hands. Quietly observe the energy you wish to banish from your personal energy field.

3 When you are ready hold the Kunzite away from you, pointing it out of the circle of light. Imagine or feel all the banished energy leaving you, draining out of your body through the Kunzite crystal.

4 When you feel all the negative energy has left you, place the Kunzite outside the circle of quartz and Labradorite crystals.

5 Imagine or feel yourself surrounded by a sphere of brilliant white healing light. Allow the light to fill your whole being, and feel your emotions rising with the light energy. Absorb as much light as you can (you should feel a warm glow inside you and perhaps even a slight rise in temperature).

6 Imagine or feel even more light being magnetized towards you. Send this energy outwards, filling the room you are in with a huge tornado of light. If you wish, send this energy further outwards to fill the whole of your home. You should now be feeling a positive surge of energy running through you.

7 To close the energy sit quietly in the centre of the circle and count your blessings. Think of all the good things in your life. Allow feelings of gratitude to fill you. The energy of gratitude attracts angels. Feel yourself surrounded by a circle of positive loving angelic beings.

8 When you feel ready, leave the circle of crystals.

Circle of light crystals

- **Labradorite** is the bringer of light that dispels darkness within the energy field. It has a vivid play of rainbow light that works on multiple levels to clear parasitic energies.

- **Kunzite** clears emotional energy that has intruded into your energy field.

- **Clear Quartz** amplifies and enhances other crystals.

Confusion

Dispelling confusion and achieving stability requires our energy to be balanced, centred, integrated and aligned. When we feel confused or ungrounded we become easily disorientated and our energies are scattered and disorganized. We appear to be in a permanent state of altered awareness and seem dreamy or distant.

People who habitually feel ungrounded are often described as inattentive, scatterbrained or daydreamers. They are often idealists who have no interest in their present situation, but live much of the time in their own fantasy worlds. These people find meditating easy and slip quickly into altered states of consciousness. Their tolerance for alcohol may be low, and it is easy for them to become addicted.

The healing process may be a cause of temporary confusion. Sometimes when people start healing their energy blocks, they become easily disorientated because of the rapid dynamic energy movements that bring changes on many levels. In order for the healing to be fully integrated and sustainable, these scattered energies must be grounded and focused.

Grounding crystals

- Smoky Quartz draws discordant energy towards itself and absorbs it. It is excellent for stabilizing the physical body. This is a wonderful grounding stone that should be used after all therapy sessions to focus energy. It prevents the condition known as a 'healing crisis' by making adapting to change and spiritual growth much easier.

- Magnetite is both grounding and energizing. It aligns the spinal column and the chakra system. By aligning our subtle-energy systems with the Earth's magnetic field, Magnetite brings security, strength and life-force renewal.

- Haematite is also an effective grounding and energizing stone that restores equilibrium and stability.

Gem essence

To avoid wandering between worlds in a state of confusion at inappropriate times, you need a crystal healing technique that will help you feel grounded. This gem essence is created from your choice of three highly effective grounding stones. You may also find that wearing or carrying one of them is beneficial.

YOU WILL NEED

1 Smoky Quartz, natural or tumbled
OR
1 Haematite, natural or tumbled
OR
1 Magnetite, natural or tumbled

WHAT TO DO

Make a gem essence (see page 14 for information on how to do this) and take it as directed.

Anger

Anger is an explosive emotional energy that relates to the fiery qualities of the solar plexus chakra. It is triggered by outside circumstances or by hormonal imbalances that overactivate this chakra. This solar fire then spills into and activates the sacral and root chakras, causing aggression, belligerence and hostility.

Anger is a by-product of fear, usually of authority figures or of situations in which we are disempowered. Our attitude towards authority figures is programmed into us as children, which is why anger is such an immature and powerful response. If those who were in authority over us during childhood abused their power by constantly criticising or punishing us, then we also developed shame for our lack of compliance. Shame blocks the solar plexus chakra because it creates feelings of disempowerment and humiliation.

Hatred occurs when the solar fire rises into the heart centre causing inner conflict. The opposite of the loving energy that normally flows from a balanced heart chakra, hatred hardens the heart and stops us relating to others with unconditional love.

Gem essence

This gem essence uses Ruby in Zoisite, a combination crystal of red Ruby and green Zoisite that is a powerful cleanser and harmonizer of the heart, solar plexus, sacral and base chakras. It transmutes the negative impulses and destructive urges of anger and hatred into constructive new behaviour patterns that are based on the wisdom of the soul rather than childish past programming. Ruby in Zoisite promotes the energy of acceptance allowing us to develop our own individuality while still honouring the interconnectedness of all life. It can also be used to facilitate past life recall.

YOU WILL NEED
1 Ruby in Zoisite, tumbled or raw

WHAT TO DO
Make a gem essence (see page 14 for information on how to do this) and take it as directed.

Ruby in Zoisite

Hyperactivity

Emotional hyperactivity can lead to fanatical behaviour patterns. Religious or lifestyle zealots have this quality in abundance. They are so emotionally charged, so totally dogmatic that their ideologies are the only ones worth having, that they will go to any lengths to convert others to their way of thinking. They use enormous emotional energy to keep going, even when their physical strength is exhausted.

People who have just discovered their personal spiritual path can suffer from hyperactivity. Their overeagerness overtakes them, they are on a mission and will force others into listening to what is good for them. This overenthusiasm can become prejudice, which stresses the emotional body.

This spiritual hyperactivity can also make those new to the metaphysical path flit from one guru or teacher to another, or try out several different complementary therapies all at the same time. Then they wonder why they develop spiritual indigestion! They suffer one healing crisis after another until finally, in total exhaustion, they learn discernment.

Lapis medicine

- Lapis (in full, Lapis Lazuli) helps you regain a state of receptive, peaceful, comprehension. Lapis opens and balances the third eye and throat chakras, which stimulates enlightened states of consciousness.

- This crystal aids discrimination and wisdom. It releases fanatical points of view that can lead to visionary and auditory hallucinations. Lapis brings objectivity and clarity, both of which are functions of the higher mind.

- Lapis also teaches the mastery of active listening by integrating both the 'inner' and outer ear. This helps you be receptive to the whisperings of your soul.

Lapis

Gem essence

Being an enthusiast for life will draw others towards your positive energy, being overenthusiastic or hyperactive will drive them away and exhaust you. You need to inspire others, not browbeat them. Learning to harmonize your energies and to use them for the best effect is essential, and this gem essence will help you to do that.

YOU WILL NEED

1 Lapis, tumbled

WHAT TO DO

Make a gem essence (see page 14 for information on how to do this) and take it as directed.

Possessiveness

Finding balance and equality in our relationships with others is not an easy task, especially if we do not love and accept ourselves unconditionally. When the heart chakra is out of balance we become needy, extremely interfering and even covertly manipulative. Love becomes a weapon that we use to coerce others into behaving or responding to our every whim (many of us will have experienced such manipulative love during childhood). At the extreme point of imbalance, self-love becomes self-pity and passive-aggressive behaviour. The paranoia of jealousy develops when we try to control everyone and every situation in life.

Emotional freedom crystals

- Hemimorphite fosters true soul expression and enhances self-esteem by teaching you to value your own individuality and the individuality of others. Wear it on your throat chakra when making decisions – it encourages self-questioning, especially about your motivation. It carries the high angelic energy of a balanced heart chakra, imbuing your energy system with emotional freedom. It is said to attract good fortune and to give protection by repelling negativity.

- Pink Sapphire is magnetic, it attracts what you need into your life, so lessons can be learned quickly. It teaches you mastery of your emotions and self-acceptance. It releases emotional baggage by neutralizing negative tendencies, and brings balance and equality to relationships by resolving misunderstandings. If you choose to wear a Pink Sapphire, it should rest against your heart chakra.

Hemimorphite

Pink Sapphire

Gem essence

This crystal healing technique will help you bring your heart chakra into balance. If you are comfortable and secure within your own heart, you will be less likely to develop possessive traits. You will see love as something to be freely given and received, not a commodity to be traded or withdrawn on a whim.

YOU WILL NEED

1 Hemimorphite, natural or tumbled
1 Pink Sapphire, natural or tumbled

WHAT TO DO

Make a combined gem essence (see page 14 for information on how to do this) and take it as directed.

Arrogance

We often unquestioningly inherit our parents' belief systems. We are also subject to social conditioning from the people around us and the media. As children or adolescents we accept this, it gives us our sense of belonging, our tribal mentality. 'Tribal mentality' alludes to your family, friends, work colleagues and any other self-limiting group who have a vested interest in your controlled behavioural patterns and in the survival of those patterns – which may serve the group, but do not necessarily serve you as an individual.

Tribal mentality can lead to arrogance. If our family or social group believe they are superior to others because of their status, wealth, nationality or religious background, then we may have been brought up to be prejudiced, hypercritical, judgmental or intolerant of others who have different backgrounds or beliefs.

An unchallenged tribal mentality frequently brings isolation for individuals and trouble between groups or nations. As we grow and mature we need to move away from this group thinking and formulate our own values of individuality and independence.

Gem essence

Used in conjunction with a self-questioning exercise, this combined gem essence will help you develop the insight that brings tolerance and appreciation of the individuality of others. It facilitates a well-grounded reality based on the wisdom of your own intuitive power and helps balance the many levels of the heart chakra with the higher chakras.

YOU WILL NEED
1 Iolite, natural or tumbled
1 Smoky Quartz, natural or tumbled

WHAT TO DO
Make a gem essence (see page 14 for information on how to do this) and take it as directed.

Smoky Quartz

Iolite

Self-questioning exercise

To understand your belief systems and past programming, you need to question your motivation and values. This is a vital step on the path to self-knowledge, individuality, independence and emotional freedom.

WHAT TO DO

1 Make a list of your beliefs. Take your time with this, and see if you can identify the root of each belief or value. Are they really yours, or have you acquired them from your parents, teachers or peer group?

2 Each belief may be seen as an energetic block, or 'thought form'. Some of these thought forms may be negative, hindering your spiritual growth, causing you unhappiness. Take the time to decide which, if any, of your beliefs do this.

3 Create a new list with two columns. Head one column 'Past Programming' and the other 'New Programming'.

4 In the Past Programming column list the values and beliefs that no longer serve your highest good. The more specific you are about the ones you wish to release, the better.

5 In the New Programming column list the new values you wish to bring into your life. Make sure these are worded in a positive way. Try phrases such as 'judgment is replaced with acceptance'; 'fear is replace with love'; 'restriction is replaced with freedom'; and 'intolerance is replaced with tolerance'.

Iolite medicine

- Iolite awakens innate inner knowledge and wisdom, it takes you into the realms of personal inner knowing, free from the expectations of those around you. It makes you more receptive to information from and communication with your higher self.

- Iolite teaches you not to get too attached to ritual, but to look for your own path using a balanced third eye chakra. This crystal strengthens intuition, aids inner balance and being centred. It improves powers of concentration and determination regardless of outside influences or circumstances.

- Iolite helps to reduce confusion by bringing us understanding of the life situation that is currently causing the problem. All confusion arises from our inability to claim our own intuitive powers and to act according to our individual needs instead of the needs of society or its restricted tribal mentality.

Iolite

Domineering attitudes

We live in a world that has been badly damaged by hard-hearted, power-crazed bullies. Some rule countries, others seize control at school, in the workplace or at home. These domineering, ruthless, cruel dictators are greedy for power and have no respect for others. Their ruthlessness comes at a price, they tend to burn themselves out and age very quickly. Domineering attitudes make extreme demands on an individual's energy field. Fear is the negative underlying emotion that spawns all the others.

All dictators have imbalanced, overactive solar plexus chakras and blighted heart chakras. Traditionally the solar plexus chakra is associated with the logical functioning of the mind. It rules our intellectual prowess, thought processes, willpower and energy manipulation on all levels. Perhaps this is the key to understanding those who become domineering – if they fail to persuade you to their way of thinking through their intellectual prowess, they resort to extreme persuasion through force.

Therapy tips

- An aversion to Malachite or the colour green indicates that we do not feel at ease with our emotions. This is usually due to childhood trauma and a dysfunctional early family background. To diagnose and clear core energy blockages within the physical and subtle bodies, use 'green healing' by placing a Malachite crystal on each master chakra centre in turn. Start with the root chakra and work upwards, finishing at the crown chakra. Spend some quiet time afterwards integrating the energetic shift facilitated by the Malachite.

- Holding an Angelite or Celestite crystal balances out the energy reformation and helps with integration of new energy patterns.

Gem essence

Equilibrium or balance is the key to a long, healthy, happy, productive life. To remain in balance we must be flexible in our attitudes. By supporting and nurturing personal and social growth we affirm the interconnectedness of all life. This gem essence will help.

YOU WILL NEED

1 Angelite, tumbled
1 Celestite, tumbled
1 Malachite, tumbled
1 Seraphinite, tumbled

NOTE: You can use either Celestite or Angelite if you don't have both crystals.

WHAT TO DO

Make a combined gem essence (see page 14 for information on how to do this) using the two containers method and take it as directed.

Victim mentality

Chronic resentment and other destructive emotions such as bitterness or sulkiness are the result of an unbalanced heart chakra. People who have attracted negative energy into their hearts feel themselves to be the hapless victims of a cruel fate. Life has it in for them. They complain endlessly with statements such as 'Life is so unfair'. It never seems to occur to them to consider their own behaviour when making such remarks. Instead they powerfully project all their resentments and disappointments onto the outside world.

These people make demands on life, but never consider what they put into it. They stress the negative aspect within any given situation and really seem to enjoy spoiling other people's positive attitudes. Suffering from the 'poor me' syndrome, they often mutter away to themselves just to build up their wall of negativity. They can carry a grudge for years, like a smouldering volcano. This unpleasant behaviour may frequently be seen in people who have passed middle age and consciously or subconsciously realized that they have little chance of fulfilling their youthful hopes, ambitions and dreams.

Those with a victim mentality often view the world through materialistic eyes. They judge success by accumulated wealth and constant youth. Outside beauty fades, and you cannot take your money or possessions with you when you die. What you can take with you is your beautiful soul, and your legacy to the world is the loving memories that your family, friends and work colleagues feel in their hearts when they think of you. Chronic resentment sufferers alienate everyone in the end, including those closest to them. Gradually grow more isolated and embittered, they end up feeling even more the victim, and leave no love behind them.

Gem essence

Recognizing your persistent negative thoughts is to take the first step on your road to recovery. Once you acknowledge just how embittered you are, that each grumbling thought is another stone in the wall of your own isolation, then you can take action. You can begin to realize that you are not a victim, but the creative architect of your own destiny. This Fuchsite gem essence will help you to release your embittered attitudes, to stop resenting what fate brings you, and to lose the feeling of being treated unjustly by life.

YOU WILL NEED
1 Fuchsite, natural

WHAT TO DO
Make a gem essence (see page 14 for information on how to do this) using the two containers method and take it as directed.

Fuchsite

Impatience

Impatience causes inner tension, stomach upsets and headaches. Developing patience is not easy, especially in today's society which is fast, furious and focused on instant gratification.

As a society we are used to instant global communications. Our senses are bombarded with new experiences, new information, all day, every day. Politicians communicate in sound bites, as their researches tell them we have a very short attention span and are easily bored thanks to the fast pace of modern advertising. We work long hours, eat fast food, sit in front of computers and televisions with telephones pressed to our ears in a sea of electrostress. Electromagnetic fields, toxins, chemicals, radio waves, power lines, radar and satellite transmissions are all around us. No wonder we feel irritable and impatient.

Curing impatience is almost impossible unless we can make small calm healing spaces in today's hectic lifestyle. We need to make time for peace and serenity, to focus inwards as well as outwards.

Therapy tips

- You may take this gem essence more frequently if necessary. If you feel acutely impatient or irritable, then take four drops every 10–20 minutes until there is an improvement.

- This gem essence can also be used in the bath – use five drops in a full bath of water.

- Crystals used in this essence can also be of benefit when placed on the chakras. Hiddenite, Green Apophyllite or Green Aventurine are soothing, calming and stabilizing when placed on the heart chakra, especially if combined with Rose Quartz, Kunzite or Pink Tourmaline. Placing Lepidolite or Amethyst on the third eye chakra frees the mind allowing detachment from emotional tension. Aquamarine when placed over the thymus eases stress and emotional debilitation.

- Try cutting down on outward stimulation. Don't put the television on the moment you come home from work, stop watching every news programme, and read fewer magazines and newspapers. Ignore your email for a few days, switch off the telephone and use the answering machine as a filter, calling people back in your own time. Stop grazing, instead take the time to savour your food, eating your meals together as a family sitting around a table. Don't race around, stop rushing to do everything at once, focus on one task at a time and work calmly with inward serenity.

- Creating a feeling of calm inside your home is important. Place crystals in any area that needs extra help. A large Amethyst geode strategically placed, especially in the entrance area, eases tension and stress throughout the whole house. Use Amethyst or Black Tourmaline near your computer, television or telephone.

Gem essence

Creating a soothing gem essence to take every day will help you unwind and relax. This essence uses pale green crystals to bring harmony and release feelings of irritability, impatience, intolerance or extreme inner tension, and combines them with pink stones to help the healing process. In addition, Moonstone and Selenite are both nurturing to the soul and stabilizing to the emotions, halting both impatience, mood swings and irritability.

YOU WILL NEED

1 Hiddenite, natural or tumbled
OR
1 Green Apophyllite, natural or tumbled
OR
1 Green Aventurine, natural or tumbled

1 Rose Quartz, natural or tumbled
OR
1 Kunzite, natural or tumbled
OR
1 Pink Tourmaline, natural or tumbled

1 Lepidolite, natural or tumbled
OR
1 Amethyst, natural or tumbled

1 Moonstone, natural or tumbled
OR
1 Selenite, natural or tumbled

1 Aquamarine, natural or tumbled

WHAT TO DO

1 Make a combined gem essence (see page 14 for information on how to do this) using the two containers method.

2 Take four drops four times daily on an empty stomach first thing in the morning, at lunch time, at about five o'clock and again at bedtime. The drops should be placed under the tongue and held in the mouth for a minute to get the full effects. The drops may also be placed in a cup of water or fruit juice and sipped slowly.

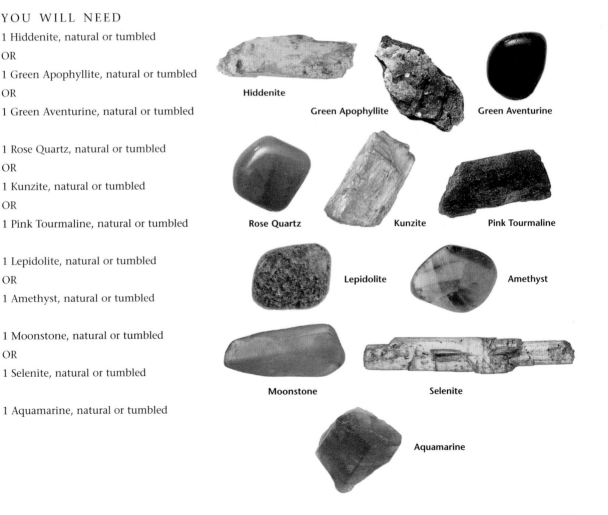

Hiddenite

Green Apophyllite

Green Aventurine

Rose Quartz

Kunzite

Pink Tourmaline

Lepidolite

Amethyst

Moonstone

Selenite

Aquamarine

Perfectionism

Nobody is perfect, but a lot of people seek both inner and outer perfection. Whilst the pursuit of excellence on all levels is to be applauded, it can cause difficulties within the personality if it becomes an obsession or a compulsion. Perfectionism without balance is a burden. Seeking perfection will cause inner conflict if we have to force ourselves through rigid physical, spiritual or mental disciplines every day to meet our self-imposed standards.

Many people on the spiritual path believe worldly desires and pursuits inhibit their spiritual development. They try too hard to develop saint-like qualities, but perfect asceticism is for monks and recluses. Many people are just too hard on themselves, which is a form of self-hatred and self-abuse. People who believe that their chosen path is the only way to salvation develop rigid mental attitudes from this conceited or self-righteous spiritual pride.

Service to others is frequently thought to be truly selfless, but often there is a hidden, even egocentric, motive. People may serve others so that they can feel useful or needed, or because they just want to look good in the eyes of others. Being a perfect martyr also stops us looking at our own faults, as we are often so busy healing others it stops us having to look at our own dis-ease.

Gem essence

Because Tiger Eye aids recognition of both talents and faults, this gem essence will help you recognize your true needs, free from your self-imposed, idealistic, rigid mental attitudes and desire for perfectionism. Life is for living and it is no eternal sin to enjoy being alive. Truly enlightened, liberated souls are joyful, even playful. Laughter is a great healer, while taking ourselves too seriously can make us appear ridiculous.

YOU WILL NEED
1 Tiger Eye, tumbled

WHAT TO DO
Make a gem essence (see page 14 for information on how to do this) and take it as directed.

Tiger eye

Addictions

Mention addiction and it is the major problems that spring to mind – drugs, alcohol, gambling, tobacco. But small-scale addictions are also signs of obsessive behaviour, and we may experience withdrawal symptoms if we fail to get our personal choice of 'fix', be it eating chocolate or watching a television soap opera at the same time every day. Many addictions are caused by thought forms. These can be self-generated, inherited or picked up from other people. Sometimes these thought forms almost take on a life of their own and may then cause severe personality disorders, obsessions and addictions.

Purple Fluorite

Amethyst

Gem essence

All violet-coloured crystals have remarkable effects. They bring balance and healing in any situation as they facilitate integration at an energetic level, removing all sorts of obstacles, blockages or addictions. They give inspiration and fire the imagination, which allows insight into fanaticism or other extremist viewpoints that can leave you vulnerable to obsessive behaviour traits.

YOU WILL NEED

1 Amethyst, natural or tumbled
1 Purple Fluorite, natural or tumbled

WHAT TO DO

Make a combined gem essence (see page 14 for information on how to do this) and take it as directed.

Violet crystals

- Amethyst was traditionally worn to prevent drunkenness because it supports sobriety. It tempers the physical passions that cause overindulgence and helps us to overcome addictions and compulsions that become obsessions. Amethyst aids integration by combining opposite energies. It enhances perception and grounds awareness.

- Amethyst allows detachment, it also detaches the negative energy that causes the blockages that result in addictive or compulsive behaviour. It

reaches deep into the body at a cellular level to remove these blockages and dependencies. Amethyst loosens the thought forms that may cause addictions and transmutes them into positive energy.

- Fluorite shares many of the qualities of Amethyst, but is especially helpful in dissolving fixed behaviour patterns. It is also excellent at restructuring chaotic energy, so allowing higher spiritual energy to be quickly integrated and absorbed. It aids discernment, impartiality and objectivity, and stops outside influences psychically manipulating your energy field.

PART 3

CRYSTALS TO STRENGTHEN YOUR SPIRIT

Crystals and your spirit

Conventional medicine focuses on the physical systems of the body. It is a scientific approach that some people feel reduces us all to a collection of chemicals or a machine. It concentrates on tests and assessments of symptoms to diagnose the problem, and aims to cure it with surgery and drugs.

This type of medicine is a comparatively recent development. Before conventional medicine became so pervasive people sought natural remedies for their ailments. They knew and understood that their lives were influenced by many different energies, some of which – the subtle-energies – cannot be seen by most people. They understood the need to heal mind and spirit as well as body.

Complementary medicine also takes this approach. It is sometimes seen as an alternative to conventional medicine, but in an ideal world we would adopt an integrated approach and look at the human condition in a holistic manner.

At the moment there is almost a desperate interest in complementary medicine, with many practitioners and journalists trying to make it appear similar to conventional medicine, offering a quick fix for every condition. This simply will never be the case, because we are all unique individuals with our own unique dis-eases and personal energy patterns.

Health, which is the freedom from dis-ease, should be viewed as the continuous harmonious flow of vital energy between the body, mind and spirit (which are collectively called the psyche). As we evolve an integrated approach we look at ourselves holistically and we begin to identify more and more with our spirit. This means we are no longer under the direct influence of the ego and the intellect. We are able to move beyond the illusion of duality and separation into the seamless bliss of soul unity within the cosmic web of life.

Crystal therapy aims to weave us back into unity with the soul. It is focused not just on wellbeing, but on so much more. It requires us to listen to the whisperings of our souls, feel our emotions, develop our intuition and nurture our spirits. This holistic state brings contentment, allowing us to function peacefully in connection with other people in the flow of life. It has integrity because it brings harmony and beauty to our life and world. It strengthens our spirits.

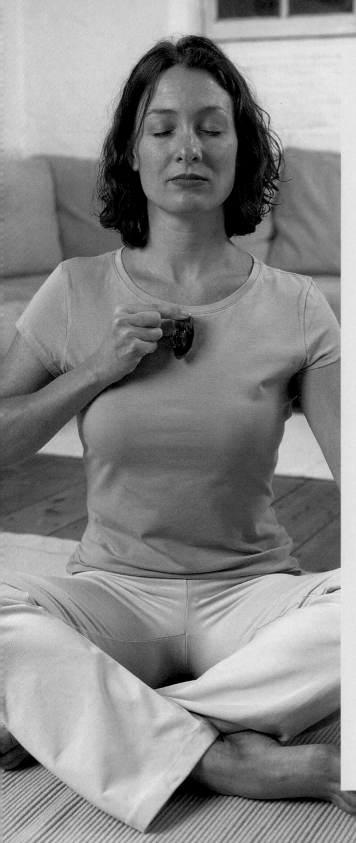

Dis-ease

- Dis-ease is a state that results from physical, emotional, mental or spiritual imbalances that cause you to be ill at ease with some aspect of yourself. It is your spirit's way of communicating with you through your physical body, your thoughts, emotions and feelings.

- Dis-ease should not be viewed as a negative experience, it is just your spirit's way of attracting your attention. When we are healthy we tend to take life for granted, we become complacent and fall into the trap of deluding ourselves that we are physically immortal. This delusion is stagnation to the soul and the death of spiritual growth.

- When dis-ease happens and you are no longer able to make sense of your life, you have the opportunity to step into the magic of living holistically. Each dis-ease and the crisis it brings as the instigator of change within your life creates a sacred space for your spirit to teach you about yourself.

- Your dis-ease is unique to you. The birth of your dis-ease is your own creation. If you grasp the opportunity of working with your soul to heal your imbalance you free yourself from a place of stagnation and move towards a more spiritual and harmonious life.

Aura balancing

All auras are different. They change constantly as our thoughts, the environment we are in and our states of health alter. Auric damage may be caused by disease, negative emotions, pollutants, addictions, stress, poor diet and breathing techniques, other people's negativity and poor spiritual hygiene.

Debris occurs within the aura when someone repeatedly holds a negative thought or addiction. Some of these thought patterns and addictions may take on a life of their own. They then influence not only the person they are attached to but may also control other people's behaviour as well.

Auric imbalances cause a loss of vitality that weakens the energy field. Energy blocks show up as dark areas in the aura. These blocks may impact on spiritual, mental, emotional or physical health.

Therapy tip

- Although any crystal can be used as an effective pendulum if it is symmetrical and comes to a point, if you are new to dowsing, you will find that a simple 5cm (2 in) long Clear Quartz pendulum is the best to use. It should be symmetrically cut and balanced, and suspended on a silver chain. It is easy to attune to this type of pendulum, and it has a broad spectrum of healing energies.

Quartz pendulum

Auric levels

- The aura consists of seven levels that correlate to the seven master chakras. Beginning with the seen (the physical body), they progress to more subtle and more refined vibrations. Each level has its own function, energy awareness and realization. Alternate layers of the aura are either fixed or moving. The first, third, fifth and seventh layers are fixed, while the second, fourth and sixth layers are moving.

- The level closest to the physical body is the **etheric level**. This is an exact fixed copy of the physical body and it is pale blue or light grey in appearance. It has tiny sparks of light within it and moves rapidly. It is a template for the physical body holding memories of the formation of the physical body.

- The **second level** relates to emotions and is a constant swirling mass of colours.

- The **third level** relates to the mental body. It is a fixed layer of yellow that holds our thought processes.

- The **fourth level** relates to our heart energy. It appears as pastel colours and when fully developed as a pastel rainbow.

- The **fifth, sixth and seventh levels** appear as bright blue, gold and silvery-blue to shimmering gold. These higher levels related to spiritual development, so are not easily observable in most people.

YOU WILL NEED

1 Clear Quartz pendulum

WHAT TO DO

1 Ask your friend to lie down comfortably, ideally where you can move around them easily.

2 Hold the pendulum just above your friend's body. Start the pendulum swinging backwards and forwards in a neutral fashion.

3 Wherever the pendulum varies from the neutral swing it has found an imbalance. Allow it to move over the imbalance until it comes back to the neutral back and forth movement. A clockwise movement means an input of energy, an anticlockwise one a release of energy.

4 Start dowsing with the centre line of the body, working from beneath the feet upwards to finish above the head. Then move to the side of your friend's body and, following the natural outline, go completely around them in a clockwise manner.

5 Work around your friend's outline once more, still in a clockwise manner, but this time about 45 cm (18 in) from the side of their body.

Aura dowsing

Many techniques exist for working in the aura but using a crystal pendulum is one of the easiest. The pendulum will seek out areas of imbalance in the aura and remove energy blocks. Dowsing can be used to energize, strengthen, align, harmonize and integrate each level of the aura. It will fill holes and stop energy leaks as well as giving protection. Practise this technique with a friend or companion, taking it in turns with them to sense any problems and to provide healing.

Chakra balancing

The seven master chakras – root, sacral, solar plexus, heart, throat, third eye and crown – lie in the centre line of the body with the first five embedded within the spinal column (see pages 18–19). These funnel-shaped swirling vortexes of energy absorb and distribute life-force, the subtle-energy known as *prana*. They are gateways or linkage-points between the various dimensions. The master chakras should always be seen as a complete integrated balanced system. Each expresses a different level of consciousness, which needs to be developed in a balanced fashion. A lack of balance in the chakra is usually caused by physical, emotional, mental or spiritual imbalance in the person affected.

Chakras in balance

- The **root chakra's** element is earth and its colour is red. Balance in this chakra is expressed as grounded, stable and reliable.

- The **sacral chakra's** element is water, and its colour is orange. Balance in this chakra is expressed as vitality, creativity and originality.

- The **solar plexus chakra's** element is fire and its colour is yellow. Balance in this chakra is expressed as logical thought processes, self-confidence and goal manifestation.

- The **heart chakra's** element is air and its colour is green. Balance in this chakra is expressed as unconditional love for ourselves and others.

- The **throat chakra's** element is ether (also written aether) and its colour is blue. Balance in this chakra is expressed as easy communication with ourselves and others on all levels

- The **third eye chakra's** element is *avyakta* (primordial cloud of undifferentiated light) and its colour is indigo. Balance in this chakra is expressed as intuition, clairvoyance, clairaudience and clairsentience.

- The **crown chakra's** element is cosmic energy and its colour is violet. Balance in this chakra is expressed as cosmic consciousness.

Balancing the chakras

This crystal healing technique suggests some suitable crystals for you to practise balancing your chakras while working on your own. A crystal therapist would normally assess the energetic quality of each of your chakras through scanning or dowsing, both before and after a balancing session. The therapist would then choose an appropriate crystal for each chakra that would correct any overactive or underactive energy flow. Crystals are usually chosen to represent the colour associated with each chakra – red, orange, yellow, green, blue, indigo and violet.

YOU WILL NEED

1 Garnet, tumbled

1 Carnelian, tumbled

1 Citrine, tumbled

1 Green Aventurine, tumbled

1 Blue Lace Agate, tumbled

1 Lapis, tumbled

1 Amethyst, tumbled

Therapy tips

- Crystals may also be placed above the head in the soul star chakra and beneath the feet in the earth star chakra. Choose clear crystals for the soul star chakra and black crystals for the earth star chakra.

- A mandala of crystals may also be placed on any chakra. An appropriate heart chakra mandala would be to arrange four pieces of Rose Quartz around the Green Aventurine.

- Crystals may also be placed around the body in the aura forming a web of light. A suitable web would be the six-crystal Star of David, made up of two interlocking triangles that form a hexagon shape around the body. For this web, choose crystals of a similar size and type such as medium size Clear Quartz with single terminations. The terminations may point inwards, to build energy, or outwards, to release energy blocks.

WHAT TO DO

1 Prepare and cleanse your crystals ready for use (see page 13 for information on how to do this).

2 Lie down comfortably on the floor, using a yoga mat or pad if you prefer.

3 Place the crystals as follows: the Garnet on your base chakra; the Carnelian on your sacral chakra; the Citrine on your solar plexus chakra; the Green Aventurine on your heart chakra; the Blue Lace Agate on your throat chakra; the Lapis on your third eye chakra; and the Amethyst on your crown chakra (see page 18 for chakra locations).

4 Allow 20 minutes for your body to integrate the energies. Be ready to remove the crystals sooner if your intuition tells that you have integrated the crystal energy more quickly.

Chakra therapy

The seven master chakras and their channels the *nadis* deal with the flow of human consciousness. The chakras are subtle-energy conductors, so this flow cannot be seen by most people. For most of us, it is easier to understand what is happening by relating the master chakras to the physical body, linking them to the glands of the endocrine system (see page 20) and to the plexuses (complex networks of nerves, blood vessels and lymph vessels) where there is a high degree of nervous activity.

Chakra correspondences

- The **root chakra** corresponds to the adrenal glands and the coccygeal nerve plexus. Malfunctions may lead to the physical problems of osteoarthritis, obesity, haemorrhoids, constipation and problems with the feet, legs, bones and teeth. Emotional and spiritual problems may include 'spaciness' and being incapable of inner stillness.

- The **sacral chakra** corresponds to the sex glands (ovaries in women, testes in men) and the sacral nerve plexus. Malfunctions may lead to the physical problems of frigidity, impotence, infertility, bladder and kidney problems, uterine disorders, prostate problems and lower back pain. Emotional and spiritual problems may include fear, shock and guilt.

- The **solar plexus chakra** corresponds to the pancreas and the solar nerve plexus. Malfunctions may lead to the physical problems of digestive disorders, diabetes and chronic fatigue. Emotional and spiritual problems may include low self-esteem, an addictive personality and aggression.

- The **heart chakra** corresponds to the thymus and the cardiac nerve plexus. Malfunctions may lead to the physical problems of lung disease, asthma, heart disease, high blood pressure, and arm, hand and finger problems. Emotional and spiritual problems may include fear of betrayal, co-dependency and melancholia.

- The **throat chakra** corresponds to the thyroid and parathyroid glands and the pharyngeal nerve plexus. Malfunctions may lead to the physical problems of stiff necks, colds, sore throats, thyroid and hearing problems and tinnitus. Emotional and spiritual problems may include perfectionism and the inability to express emotions.

- The **third eye chakra** corresponds to the pituitary gland and the carotid nerve plexus. Malfunctions may lead to the physical problems of headaches, nightmares, eye problems, neurological disturbances and glaucoma. Emotional, spiritual and mental problems may include learning difficulties and hallucinations.

- The **crown chakra** corresponds to the pineal gland and the cerebral cortex nerve plexus. Malfunctions may lead to confusion, depression, obsessional thinking, sensitivity to pollutants, chronic exhaustion, epilepsy and dementia.

Chakra therapy visualization

The health of your chakras is important for the health of your mind, body and spirit – your psyche. This crystal healing technique helps you to correct any overactivity or underactivity in the flow of the subtle-energies. Although simple, this technique may take up to 60 minutes the first time you practise it. The time needed depends entirely on the health of your chakras and subsequent sessions will often be shorter.

YOU WILL NEED

2 Boji stones® (1 male, 1 female)

WHAT TO DO

1. Prepare and cleanse your Boji stones® (see page 13 for information on how to do this).

2. Lie down comfortably on the floor, using a yoga mat or pad if you prefer.

3. Hold the female stone in your left hand and the male in your right hand. Allow your eyes to close. Breathe deeply for 5 minutes to bring oxygen to your brain.

4. Turn your full attention to each of your master chakras in turn (see page 18 for their locations), beginning with the root chakra. Visualize the flow of energy. As you focus on each chakra, simply be aware of the subtle-energy movement, try not to control the movement, just be aware of it.

5. Allow the Boji stones® to activate, open, cleanse, heal (to calm or energize or strengthen or reform as needed), align, harmonize and integrate each master chakra in sequential order, finishing with the crown chakra.

6. Slowly and gently allow yourself to return to everyday physical reality.

Balancing the meridians

Life-force or *chi* flows through channels known as meridians (see page 17). There are 12 major meridians that run down the body in pairs, plus two extra that run up the torso and head on the front and back. Each meridian has a start and end point, which indicate direction of flow and function. They do not run in straight lines, but flow near the surface of the skin. They are named after their corresponding *yin* and *yang* organs or their function (see below). Illness or pain occur when the meridians become blocked, overactive or underactive, thereby disrupting the flow of *chi* and breaking the body's harmony.

Meridian locations

- The **central meridian** is the main *yin* channel. It begins at the perineum, flows up the front centre of the body and ends below the lower lip.

- The **governing meridian** is the main *yang* channel. It begins at the perineum, flows up the back centre of the body, over the top of the head and back down to the centre of the upper lip.

- The **gall bladder meridian** is a descending *yang* pathway. It begins at the outer edge of the eye and ends at the outer end of the fourth toe.

- The **liver meridian** is an ascending *yin* pathway. It begins at the outside of the big toe and ends just above the bottom of the ribcage.

- The **bladder meridian** is a descending *yang* pathway. It beings at the inner canthus of the eye (where the upper and lower eyelids meet) and ends on the outer edge of the little toe.

- The **kidney meridian** is an ascending *yin* pathway. It begins at the ball of the foot and ends where the collarbone and breastbone meet.

- The **large intestine meridian** is an ascending *yin* pathway. It begins at the outer edge of the nostril and ends on the inner edge of the index finger.

- The **lung meridian** is an ascending *yin* pathway. It begins just below the coracoid process (a peg-like structure on the shoulder blade) and ends on the inner end of the thumb.

- The **stomach meridian** is a descending *yang* pathway. It begins below the eye at the inner edge of the eye socket and ends at the outer end of the second toe.

- The **spleen meridian** is an ascending *yin* pathway. It begins at the inner edge of the big toe and ends at the side of the chest just below nipple level.

- The **small intestine meridian** is a descending *yang* pathway. It begins at the outer end of the little fingertip and ends at the start of the upper edge of the ear in a small hollow of the cheek.

- The **triple heater meridian** is a descending *yang* pathway. It begins at the outside end of the ring (third) finger and ends at the outer edge of the eyebrow.

- The **heart meridian** is a descending *yang* pathway. It begins at the front edge of the armpit and ends at the inner edge of the little finger.

- The **pericardium meridian** is an ascending *yin* pathway. It begins at the outer edge of the nipple and finishes on the inside of the middle finger.

Meridian cleansing

Once you have identified which meridians are dysfunctional, it is easy to bring them back into balance. The Chinese use acupuncture, the Japanese use shiatsu, while crystal therapists place gemstones at the start or end point of a meridian. Each technique strengthens, disperses or calms *chi*.

YOU WILL NEED

1 Clear Quartz pendulum

1 Citrine, natural or tumbled

1 Amethyst, natural or tumbled

1 Blue Lace Agate, natural or tumbled

NOTE If you don't have Citrine, you can use Carnelian, Zincite or Ruby instead. You can use Magnetite instead of Amethyst, and Celestite and Blue Calcite are both suitable alternatives for Blue Lace Agate.

WHAT TO DO

1 Use the Clear Quartz pendulum to dowse over a list of the meridians to identify any that are out of balance.

2 Continue dowsing to identify if the *chi* needs to be strengthened, dispersed or calmed. Select your crystal accordingly, choosing Citrine for strengthening, Amethyst for dispersing or Blue Lace Agate for calming *chi*.

3 Dowse to discover whether you should place the crystal at the start or end of the meridian, and for the length of time the placement should last.

4 Place the chosen crystal on the meridian and leave it in place for the appropriate length of time. Hold the crystal in place with surgical tape if necessary.

Element balancing

When the Greek philosopher Plato wrote *Timaeus* (his dialogue on cosmology) he sought to symbolically interpret the formation of the world through geometry. He was searching for the sacred building blocks of creation and their relationship with the elements of fire, earth, air and water. He arrived at five basic geometric forms that he considered to represent the only way the smallest indivisible parts of these elements could pack together to create the physical universe out of chaos.

Plato determined that the four basic elements of fire, earth, air and water were respectively related to four basic regular forms – the tetrahedron, cube, octahedron and icosahedron. He also explored a 'fifth' element called 'aether' that he associated with the dodecahedron. In fact these five forms are the only three-dimensional solids possible that are bounded by flat surfaces (faces) that all have exactly the same shape and size. The tetrahedron has four faces (all triangles), the hexahedron (cube) six faces (all squares), and so on.

Platonic solids

- The **hexahedron** or cube has six faces (all squares) and is related to the element of earth, the root chakra and the colour red. It releases fears by strengthening the practical aspect of your nature, bringing harmony, stability, inner strength, spontaneity and support. It will also help to bring your plans and wishes to fruition.

- The **icosahedron** has 20 faces (all triangles) and is related to the element of water, the sacral chakra and the colour orange. It heightens communication with your subconscious, easing irrational fears and past trauma, and allowing feelings of joy, laughter and delight to flow. It also enhances dream recall, psychic development and telepathic communication.

- The **tetrahedron** has four faces (all triangles) and is related to the element of fire, the solar plexus chakra and the colour yellow. It is dynamic, tonifying, strengthening and warming, bringing purification and renewing passion for life. It helps you build safe and effective energetic boundaries and to channel any angry emotions into positive pursuits.

- The **octahedron** has eight faces (all triangles) and is related to the element of air, the heart chakra and the colour green. It focuses on lightness, airiness and freedom of movement. Before we can really be as 'light as air' we need to free up our energy. There is no greater way of freeing energy than by practising forgiveness and unconditional love for ourselves and others.

- The **dodecahedron** has 12 faces (all pentagons) and is related to the element of aether, the throat chakra and the colour blue. It focuses on integrating the energies of the higher self. This is accomplished through spiritual transformation and inspiration. Balance, equilibrium and deep healing are initiated as feelings of inner emptiness are released.

Balancing the body's five elements

Combining the master-healer Clear Quartz with each of the five Platonic solids in turn creates a powerful crystal healing technique that can be used to balance the elements and the chakras. You can support this technique with a meditation exercise. If you have a set of these solids fashioned from Clear Quartz it would be beneficial to explore their elemental healing potential during meditation by holding each geometric shape in turn.

YOU WILL NEED

6 medium-sized Clear Quartz, with single terminations

WHAT TO DO

1 Lie down comfortably on the floor, using a yoga mat or pad if you prefer.

2 Place each geometric form around your physical body. Start with the hexahedron (cube) and work through each geometric form in turn.

3 For the hexahedron (cube), place four Clear Quartz as a square around your body. For the icosahedron, arrange six of the crystals around you as a six-pointed star (effectively two interlocking triangles). The tetrahedron requires three Clear Quartz arranged around you in a triangle (with its point above your head) and the octahedron four crystals arranged in an equilateral cross. For the dodecahedron, place five Clear Quartz in a five-pointed star around you (again with the point above your head).

4 Allow yourself 5 minutes in each geometric form to begin with, gradually building up to 15 minutes in each as you gain more confidence.

5 Start each session with each form with the terminations of the crystals pointing towards your body, then after a few minutes turn them to point away from you. See if you can detect a change in the energy.

Absent healing

Understanding how and why absent or distant healing works requires us to acknowledge the subtle-energy that permeates our universe. Everyone exists on several levels of reality at the same time and all energy comes from a single Source (which we may call God). As the Source is outside the reality of space and time and is on all levels simultaneously, 'it' is not subject to 'normal' scientific laws. When we raise our awareness from the purely physical plane we can step outside the rigid physical patterns and influence the flow of energy instantaneously. This is why the power of prayer is so effective – it is a method of influencing the cosmic currents to flow in a particular direction.

Absent healing can be used for single individuals or large groups, even entire nations. Many people wish to help others, especially after seeing the terrible situations that plague our world. People feel burdened by these visions of unimaginable human suffering and seek to offer relief. When sending planetary healing, suppressing your emotions causes blockages in the subtle bodies that may affect your health. Instead, focus fully on the emotions that the haunting images created within you. This eases the feelings of distress you are holding and directs the healing energy to where it is needed most.

Animals can also benefit from absent healing. They can suffer from a wide range of diseases and, just like humans, are subject to environmental pollutants, bad diets and stress. Because they are empathic, they will absorb their owner's emotional problems. Animals do not have the same rigid beliefs as humans, so they are open and willing to change and quickly integrate healing energy.

Therapy tips

- You should ideally ask the recipient for permission before sending healing. As this is not always possible, let your intuition and conscience guide you to be sure that you are behaving ethically. Similarly, always send healing without any attachments as to the outcome.

- Allow the benefits of absent healing to continue after you have finished your healing session by placing your crystal on top of a photograph of the recipient or on a piece of paper on which you have written their name. This works best if your crystal is a pyramid or a standing point. Alternatively, place a triangular web of programmed crystals around the photograph.

Amethyst

Distance healing

This is not only a powerful way of working with crystals but also a good way of developing your awareness of the healing currents that surrounds us. You may find that it helps your focus to have a picture of the person to whom you are sending the healing, or something of theirs to hold, or even just their name written on a piece of paper. This could be particularly useful if you are sending healing to someone you have never actually met.

YOU WILL NEED

1 Clear Quartz, with single termination

OR

1 Amethyst, with single termination

WHAT TO DO

1 Program the crystal for absent healing (see page 12 for information on how to do this). Sit comfortably on a chair with your feet firmly on the floor. Imagine roots growing out of the soles of your feet to ground you. Visualize yourself surrounded by a protective cocoon of brilliant white light.

2 Allow your breathing to be easy and natural. Sit quietly and focus your mind on the person to whom you are sending the healing.

3 Hold your crystal in your right hand, termination facing away from you. Visualize a beam of the white light emanating from the tip of your crystal. Continue focussing and you will feel a definite contact being made with the person (this may take a few minutes to happen).

4 Allow the beam of light from the crystal to make a very strong contact with the person you are healing. Once this contact is established allow the healing to flow. This usually takes about 20 minutes.

5 Hold your concentration on the person, as the more you focus the stronger the energy will be. Be aware of any insights you receive into the reason for their dis-ease. You may also send them positive loving thoughts.

6 When you have finished sending healing, retract the white light into the crystal. Ground and centre yourself, and cleanse your crystal.

Space clearing

The feelings of relaxation and renewal that creating a small calm area – a sacred space – within your home brings is well worth the effort required. The soul can then make itself heard in an atmosphere of peace and tranquillity. If you have a sanctuary room, so much the better, but even a small space that you can keep clutter-free and where you can place objects you find inspiring will have a calming influence on your life. Even a small shelf, window ledge or table can become an altar.

Anywhere that you can place inspirational objects can offer valuable grounding for your spirituality. Objects should be pleasing and emotionally uplifting, such as crystals, candles, angelic art, photographs of loved ones, incense, flowers, aromatherapy oils, religious icons or feathers. Remember to place a representation of anything you wish to attract into your life, such as love, spiritual wisdom, or abundance. The beauty of crystals makes them a natural choice for decorating your sacred space. Large crystal groups attract your gaze and hold your attention while the mind relaxes.

Therapy tips

- If you are the type of person who is easily drained by the constant and unnatural demands of modern environments, then you should repeat this cleansing technique at regular intervals.

- If you are cleansing someone else's house, it would be wise to put your protection around you before you enter.

- If you are cleansing all through a house then draw a figure-of-eight in the centre of each room as you clear it to close, seal and protect the space.

With our increasingly busy lives we all need time for reflection and calm. Our sacred space need not be indoors, or even be a physical place. Through meditation and visualization techniques we can create our own healing sanctuary on the inner planes of our mind.

Energetic cleansing

Before you can create your sacred space you need not only to physically clean your home and remove any clutter but also remove any stagnant energy. This crystal healing technique dynamically clears and releases spaces with built-up negative emotional, psychic and mental energies. Before beginning, make sure that your crystal is suitably cleansed and programmed (see pages 12–13 for information on how to do this).

YOU WILL NEED
1 large Clear Quartz crystal

Clear Quartz

WHAT TO DO

1 Open a window to allow the stagnant energy an exit route. Alternatively, dispose of such energy with a violet flame visualization or a large Amethyst cluster.

2 Stand in the centre of the room you are cleansing. If purifying the whole house, start in an upstairs room and work in a methodical manner throughout the house, finishing at the main entrance.

3 Hold your Clear Quartz crystal in your right hand and visualize yourself surrounded by a protective cocoon of brilliant white light. Focus, centre and ground yourself.

4 Take several deep connected breaths and begin to bring the clearing balancing energies of this brilliant white light down through your crown chakra and down through your body until you feel the energies flowing strongly throughout your entire body. Check to make sure the energies are flowing freely and strongly.

5 Send these energies of clearing, balance and harmony out of the point of your Clear Quartz crystal, slowly filling the entire room. You can use a sweeping motion over the whole space, or direct the energies towards the areas that your intuition tells you are the more stagnant.

6 Your intuition will tell you when the process is complete. It may take several minutes, or happen in seconds, or require over an hour, depending on the negativity and disharmony of the space.

7 Close, seal and protect the space with a figure-of-eight drawn in the centre of the room.

8 Check to make sure you are once more focused, centred, grounded and protected. Cleanse your crystal.

Removing spirit attachments

If your aura is damaged you may be open to the misery of spirit attachments (also known as negative entities or parasites). A damaged aura may be caused by disease, negative thoughts, pollutants, addictions, stress, psychic attack, emotional turmoil, inadequate diet, poor breathing techniques or poor spiritual cleanliness. Holes, gaps and tears within the aura are also very common, much more so than most people realize, and they may result in multiple energy leakages causing debilitation.

If the integrity of your aura becomes damaged you may attract negative entities that affect your life-force. Attachments are usually created by outside causes, for example when one individual damages another it causes energy leakage. Spirit attachments may also cause you to behave in a manner that is out of character. Such changes can be subtle or dramatic and often involve a 'new' addiction. Addictions and negative thought patterns may take on a life of their own and act as a form of possession.

Therapy tips

- To raise the receptiveness in your hands, wash them in cool water and dry them thoroughly. Sensitize your hands by shaking them vigorously (this releases blocked energy). Then rub your palms together rapidly in a circular motion several times to build up the surface *chi*. Alternatively, roll a Clear Quartz crystal between your palms.

- As you work through all the levels of your friend's aura looking for debris, you will find it helpful to use both your hands together as a diagnostic tool. This will give you a clear definition of the shape and size of the problem.

- Debris will normally penetrate through more than one level of the aura. If there are attachments, you may find you need to trace them back to the connection point.

- Holes, tears and gaps in the aura normally feel hollow or empty.

- Intuitive sensing (scanning) of someone's energy field is know as subtle-body attunement. You can use this technique to create an energetic profile that will help you to choose appropriate crystals for the person being scanned.

Auric repair

If you are working alone, on yourself, you can use this technique to sense and repair minor damage to your aura. However, it would be better to get together with a friend or companion so that you can work with the whole aura.

You can then take it in turns to sense any hurts or attachments, and to provide healing with Labradorite. This crystal is the 'bringer of light' that dispels darkness within the energy field. It has a vivid play of rainbow light that works on multiple levels to clear parasitic energies.

YOU WILL NEED

Several Labradorite, tumbled

WHAT TO DO

1 Ask your friend to lie face up, ideally on a therapy couch. Arms and legs should not be crossed during the crystal healing because that will block the energy flow.

2 Take a deep breath and relax yourself. Visualize yourself surrounded by a protective cocoon of brilliant white light. Still your mind, focus completely on your friend.

3 Remaining non-judgmental and positive throughout, allow yourself several minutes to gain energetic rapport. This attunement process is vital, especially when you practise this technique with someone for the first time. In subsequent sessions, you can reduce the attunement time.

4 You will be sensing the energetic integrity and overall structure of your friend's aura with your palm chakras. You can use either your left or right hand or both hands simultaneously. Whichever you choose, remember to keep your palm chakras pointing towards your friend.

5 Start at the feet and work upwards. Learn to trust your intuition. Place a Labradorite wherever you feel low energy, debris or similar damage. Leave it in place for a few minutes until your intuition tells you it has completed its work. Scan the area again to check that there has been an improvement.

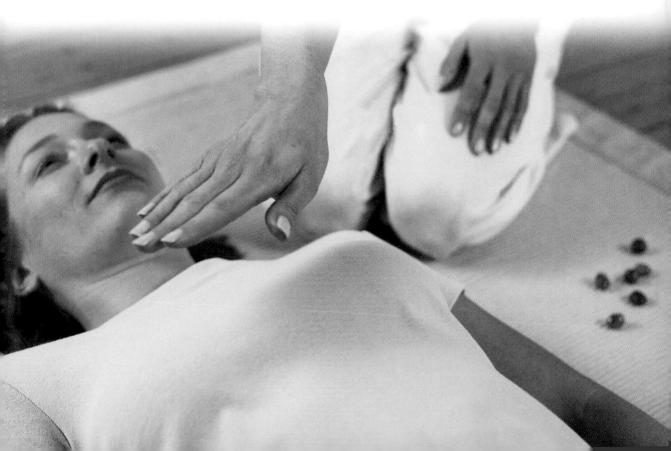

Breaking ties

Negative attachments not only weaken the spirit but starve the body of vital life-force, causing a lack of mental focus, lethargy or feelings of overwhelming despair. They also block our creativity and personal development. Releasing these attachments or binding ties is known as tie-breaking.

Some attachments are designed to control us emotionally, others sexually, physically, mentally or spiritually. Energy vampirism is very common. These vampires feed off our energy – we all know people whose company we enjoy but who leave us feeling exhausted. Normally vampire attachments are through our solar plexus chakra, but any chakra can affected. Some attachment hooks may begin by going into one chakra but are then woven on into several more.

People who are empathic can also inadvertently absorb other people's emotions, which causes psychic debilitation. If this happens to you, then you may find strengthening your aura helpful (see page 118).

We can also tie ourselves up in emotional knots by holding on to old relationships, past suffering, trauma or abuse. This binds a lot of our energy and we need to free this energy in order to move forwards. Emotional baggage slows us down, it builds up over the years causing unresolved emotional stress and blockages within our energy system, which weakens our energy field.

Tie–breaking web

This is a powerful technique, and tie-breaking can be a very emotional experience. It takes time and patience, so allow your body, mind and spirit plenty of time to integrate the new energetic patterns. You may also find it helpful to work with a close friend that you trust.

YOU WILL NEED

6 Kyanite blades

NOTE You will need the blue form of Kyanite for this technique.

WHAT TO DO

1 Lie down comfortably on the floor, using a yoga mat or pad if you prefer.

2 Place four Kyanite blades around your body, one above your head, one beneath your feet and one each side of your body at your elbows. Place the fifth blade underneath your head at the base of your skull and the sixth on your third eye chakra (between and just above your eyes).

3 Start by using your intuition to scan your subtle bodies with the clear intention of discovering any attachments. As soon as you identify one, visualize a small figure-of-eight over the area (which may be a master chakra or any other area on the body). You will feel the attachment's hook releasing and the attachment itself breaking apart and then either disintegrating or detaching from your body and aura. If the attachement is proving difficult to remove, just mentally use the word 'release'.

4 Once the attachment is removed, visualize white light filling the space where it has been to close, seal and protect.

5 Repeat the process until you have removed all attachments or as many as you can cope with in one session.

6 Finish the session by visualizing a circle of brilliant white light around your body to close, seal and protect your energy field. A circle represents psychic wholeness and unity. Remove the crystals.

7 Spend 20 minutes resting to allow your body to integrate the energies.

Kyanite medicine

- Kyanite (also called Disthene) grows in flat blade crystals that often have striations (parallel scratches or grooves) along their length. A Kyanite blade has a very focused swift action that is augmented by these striations. They allow the crystal to move energy swiftly between the chakra linkage points, which releases energy blocks, ties, hooks and ensnarements.

- Kyanite restores your energy balance and integrates your body's energies. With conscious attunement, it aligns all the chakras and activates their linkage points, which balances and strengthens the subtle bodies.

- Kyanite's metaphysical name is the sword of truth. As the seeker of truth it enhances psychic abilities, intuition and inner guidance.

Kyanite

Healing the inner child

Traumatic experiences in early childhood deeply influence the adult that the child becomes, but become buried in the recesses of the body, mind and spirit (psyche). The inner child is a universal archetype that, when approached, brings not only the release of dis-ease and restriction within the adult but also an outpouring of hope and creativity for the future.

The evolution of each of your seven master chakras represents a unique stage of growth. If any of these chakra milestones are not properly achieved, it will cause that chakra to remain in a state of underdevelopment. Healing the inner child brings inspiration and renewal for any chakras that remain left behind.

Chakra evolution

- The **root chakra** relates to conception, the formation of the physical body and birth. Your immediate needs were for survival, food, warmth and shelter.

- The **sacral chakra** evolves from 6 months to 2 years of age. Your needs were enjoyment and gratification.

- The **solar plexus chakra** develops from about 18 months to 3 years of age. Its development is associated with early socializing and the learning of language.

- The **heart chakra** evolves from 3 years to 7 years of age. It learns through relationships with the outside world.

- The **throat chakra** develops from 7 years of age onwards. Its evolution is the expression of the self.

- The **third eye chakra** starts to evolve from 12 years of age. This chakra learns through discernment and discrimination which gives insight. It evaluates the actions of others and belief systems.

- The **crown chakra** has no particular development age. It may remain dormant in some individuals as it deals with the spiritual quest to find God.

Inner child visualization

This technique is very fluid and you need to be willing to go with the flow. If during the course of your visualization you make a promise to your inner child, then you must keep it. It may be helpful to write it down, along with anything else you felt or discovered. Meditation experiences can dissipate like dreams unless they are written down, which brings them into the physical realm.

YOU WILL NEED

1 Clear Quartz, with single termination
1 Smoky Quartz, with single termination
1 Smithsonite, natural or tumbled

NOTE: You will need the pink-lavender form of Smithsonite for this technique.

Clear Quartz

Smoky Quartz

Smithsonite

WHAT TO DO

1 Before starting the visualization, cleanse all the crystals (see page 13 for information on how to do this).

2 Lie down comfortably on the floor, using a yoga mat or pad if you prefer.

3 Place the Clear Quartz, termination upwards, above your crown chakra. Place the Smoky Quartz, termination downwards, between your feet. Place the Smithsonite on your heart chakra (see page 18).

4 Close your eyes and allow your body to relax, starting at the feet and working upwards.

5 Think about how life was for you as a child. Use your intuition to contact your inner child and invite him or her to come to you. This may take several minutes.

6 Visualize or view your inner child, evaluate how your inner child looks and feels. Is it how you expected? Is your inner child a boy or a girl?

7 Ask your inner child if anything is troubling him or her and if or how you can help. You may be asked to explore new creative pursuits, or you may be shown a past experience that has hurt you. If it feels appropriate go back to the

experience and change the outcome. Maybe you will just be there for the child you once were, perhaps to give a reassuring hug or to offer some words of comfort or advice.

8 When your intuition tells you the time is right, open your eyes and remove the crystals.

Miasms

Miasms are subtle-energy imprints. You could think of them as 'crystallized patterns' that can lodge in any of the subtle body systems and cause disease or illness. The term 'miasm' was first used by Samuel Hahnemann, the founder of homeopathy. There are four basic types: karmic, acquired, inherited and planetary.

Karma is a Sanskrit word meaning the sum total of a person's actions in this and previous lives. The karmic principle allows each person to experience the full scope of all perspectives on life. It is central to all Eastern religions and similar principles are also found in Western religions. For example, Christianity teaches that you should 'do unto others as you would have others do unto you'. Karmic miasms are the residue of past life actions that lodge in the etheric body and have the potential to develop into illness, dis-ease or suffering in the present life or future lives. This predisposition often determines our attitude and behaviour in this lifetime.

Acquired miasms are acute or infectious diseases or petrochemical toxicity acquired during this lifetime. After the acute phase of an illness, these miasmatic traits settle into the subtle bodies, where they predispose you to other related illnesses.

Inherited miasms can also be called hereditary miasms. These subtle-energy imprints are passed down to you from your ancestors. They may be genetic, or can be from infectious diseases such as TB or syphilis.

Planetary miasms are stored in the collective consciousness of the planet in the etheric level. They may penetrate the physical body or subtle bodies.

Therapy tips

- This web can be used to explore your past lives. To do this, lie within the web with the Amethyst terminations all facing inwards for a maximum of 20 minutes. Ground yourself thoroughly afterwards with Smoky Quartz, Haematite or Black Tourmaline.

- Moldavite activates visionary skills, and you can add more pieces of Moldavite to this web as your vibrational rate rises. Placing Moldavite on the heart, throat and crown chakras as well as replacing the Amethyst crystals with Moldavite brings full activation of your light body. Once your light body is fully anchored in the physical body you will have access to all your past lives and be able to clear all karmic miasms.

Clearing miasms crystals

- Amethyst is a transformational healer that brings spiritual growth and understanding. It purifies all the subtle bodies. When consciously directed it will break down and transform miasms, stagnant energy and addictions. It draws out pain and gives protection during meditation.

- Moldavite is a transformational stone from the stars, a Tektite that came to Earth over 15 million years ago. It can take you into uncharted realms of infinite possibilities. Metaphysically speaking, we have within us the light body and this contains encodements of information-like files. When we hold Moldavite this data is released. Many people are not consciously aware of the information being unlocked, they just feel a huge wave of powerful energy that actually surges through the body.

Clearing miasms

Although this web can be used for all types of miasms, it is particularly effective for karmic miasms. Remember to cleanse and purify the crystals you use for this web both before and after use (see page 13 for information on how to do this) to ensure they hold the maximum of positive energy.

YOU WILL NEED

12 Amethysts, with single terminations
1 Moldavite crystal

WHAT TO DO

1 Lie down comfortably on the floor, using a yoga mat or pad if you prefer.

2 Place the Amethyst around your body, one above your head, one beneath your feet and five on each side of your body, evenly spaced.

3 Place the Moldavite on your third eye, which lies between and just above your physical eyes.

4 Remain in the web for 10 minutes with the Amethyst terminations facing inwards, then for 10 minutes with them facing outwards.

5 Ground and centre yourself afterwards by holding a Black Tourmaline or Smoky Quartz crystal in your hand.

Phobias

Your subconscious mind is very important, it is the part that looks after you on a second-by-second basis. It is responsible for your total wellbeing and survival. Your memories and the way you respond to people and situations have been learned by and stored in your subconscious. Change your subconscious programming and you change the way you respond to people and situations.

Phobias and post-traumatic stress disorder (PTSD) are anxiety disorders that have not been processed properly by your brain. They have a strong emotional response. The key to releasing them lies in the subconscious mind, in clearing the emotion that is the trigger for the phobia or PTSD. No trigger means no response, and the subconscious mind is released to process the memory in the correct way.

Smoky Quartz medicine

- Smoky Quartz is an excellent meditation stone. It allows for clarity of thought and deep contemplation.

- Smoky Quartz draws discordant energy towards itself and absorbs it. Carrying Smoky Quartz keeps you grounded in fearful situations.

- Smoky Quartz is a wonderful grounding stone and should be used after all energy work to ground and focus your energy to prevent the condition know as a healing crisis.

Smoky Quartz

Clearing phobias

This technique uses Smoky Quartz, which draws the strong emotional response from the phobia towards itself and absorbs it. The crystal healing of the Smoky Quartz is supported by meditation, which balances both hemispheres of the brain and which also helps your conscious and unconscious mind work better together.

YOU WILL NEED
1 Smoky Quartz, with single termination

WHAT TO DO

1 Prepare and cleanse your Smoky Quartz (see page 13 for information on how to do this).

2 Sit comfortably on the floor with your legs crossed. Place the crystal at your left side. Place your hands in your lap, with your right hand resting on your left. Allow your eyes to close.

3 Begin with 5 minutes of deep breathing to bring oxygen to your brain. Then slow your breathing and turn your full attention to the

movement of your breath. Do not try to control your breathing, simply be aware of the breath entering and leaving your body.

4 With your right hand, tap your witness point three times. Your witness point is located on your breastbone between your heart and your throat. Return your right hand to your lap and become aware of your witness point. You may feel a tingling sensation as it begins to activate.

5 Pick up your Smoky Quartz, hold it in your right hand with the termination pointing downwards (towards the ground) and gently hold the crystal to your witness point. Think about the phobia you have chosen to release. Feel all the emotions associated with the experience and bring the full memory into your conscious awareness. Allow the distress to well up in your body.

6 What will happens next is nothing short of astonishing. Suddenly you will feel all the anxiety attached to the phobia draining away from your conscious and subconscious mind. Your emotions will become calm.

7 Keep holding the Smoky Quartz at the witness point. Often you will feel another surge of energy as the crystalline structure goes even deeper into your subconscious mind to draw out the painful emotions. This surging feeling may occur several times as your body releases the memory and the strong emotional trigger that is attached to the experience. Each time you feel the surge, be aware that your body has chosen to release at a deeper level.

Therapy tip

- An Obsidian sphere can be substituted for the Smoky Quartz in this technique. Obsidian is the 'warrior of truth' that draws hidden imbalances to the surface to release them. It teaches us to let go of our limitations and self-imposed restrictions.

Obsidian sphere

Soul loss

Sometimes deeply traumatic events or acute or prolonged ill health can make us feel ill at ease within ourselves. It is as if we have lost a part of ourselves. We can view these as times of darkness or the 'dark night of the soul', when we feel without hope and no light is entering into our lives. Sometimes these feelings of loss of the self may be due to soul loss, soul fragmentation or soul shock. The path of recovery on a soul level has been called 'soul retrieval'. By developing spiritual insight we acknowledge and accept how we feel. This allows the light of the soul to flood through our being to summons all aspects of our soul back into a unified whole. Soul-retrieval practitioners journey to other dimensions to retrieve soul fragments.

Soul retrieval web

In this web the Clear Quartz crystals placed around your body unify the subtle-energy field and attract positive life-force, so supporting the crystal healing properties of the other three stones. This technique should be used at any time when you feel ill at ease within yourself. It can also be used to for spiritual development and light body activation.

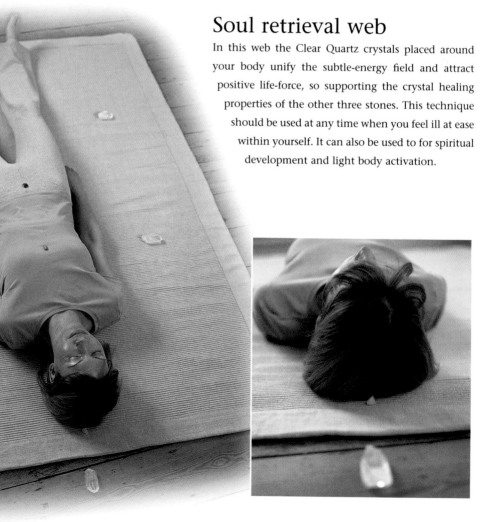

YOU WILL NEED

6 Clear Quartz, with single terminations

1 Phenacite, natural

1 Rubellite, natural or tumbled

1 Ruby, tumbled

WHAT TO DO

1 Prepare and cleanse all your crystals (see page 13 for information on how to do this).

2 Lie down comfortably on the floor, using a yoga mat or pad if you prefer.

3 Place the Clear Quartz crystals around your body, one above your head, one beneath your feet and two at each side of your body, at your knees and your elbows. Allow the crystal energy to flow around you.

4 Place the Phenacite crystal just above your head in the crown chakra, the Rubellite on your heart chakra and the Ruby on your root chakra (see page 18 for the locations of the chakras).

5 Allow your eyes to close. Begin with 5 minutes of deep breathing to bring oxygen to your brain. Then slow your breathing and turn your full attention to the movement of your breath. Do not try to control your breathing, simply be aware of the breath entering and leaving your body.

6 Allow 20 minutes for your body to integrate the energies. Be ready to remove the crystals sooner if your intuition tells that you have integrated the crystal energy more quickly.

Soul retrieval crystals

- Phenacite is a rare crystal with a very high vibration. It is a powerful activator of the upper chakras, especially the crown chakra and the non-physical eighth to fourteenth chakras above the head. The soul star chakra, which is situated just above the crown chakra, becomes especially energized and this allows any soul fragments to be reintegrated.

- Phenacite aids the ascension process by activating the light body. It purifies the chakra centres, which helps you consciously to experience higher dimensions. It encourages the development of wisdom, understanding, truth, discrimination, serenity, self-restraint, mental focus, fortitude, patience and forgiveness.

- Phenacite aids astral travel and initiates contact with ascended masters and angelic guides for those who choose to work in this way. Clear-faceted stones work the best but, as with all crystal healing techniques, your intent and dedication will bring good results, regardless of the clarity.

- Rubellite provides powerful strengthening to the heart chakra. It encourages the development of wisdom, empathy and compassion. It enhances your appreciation of the beauty all around you.

- Ruby renews your passion for life, truth, courage, wisdom and perseverance. It emits the energy of cheerfulness and stops unwanted outside sources draining your energy.

Phenacite   Ruby

Angelic attunement

Angels are winged messengers. The name is derived from the Greek word *angelos*, which means messenger. Angels and archangels act as channels for the higher refined emanations of God.

Your guardian angel is your personal helper who has sustained you through all your incarnations and faithfully records all your actions. This angel will help you through all your trials and tribulations, bringing comfort, consolation and encouragement. Although you may have heard a gentle voice encouraging you in times of personal crisis or despair, your guardian angel can never interfere with your free will.

Angelic contact crystals

- Angelite is a heavenly blue crystal that brings peace, tranquillity, calm and focus to the highest realms of heavenly angelic light.

- Celestite allows you to journey freely to the celestial realms to find inspiration and joy.

- Danburite carries a very high vibration that stimulates the third eye and crown chakras, plus the transcendental chakras in the etheric body. This connects you to the communication currents of the angelic domain.

- Seraphinite activates angelic contact in the highest realms of love, light and healing. It brings balance and stability to the heart chakra and aligns it with the crown chakra.

- Selenite is a stone of communication and communion with our celestial guides and angels. It aids telepathic links with others by enhancing intuitive and remote viewing skills.

Attune to your guardian angel

Contact with your guardian angel is always positive, bringing feelings of peace and emotional well-being. This crystal healing technique uses Angelite to bring angelic love and harmony into your life. Angelic communion is enhanced during this meditation as your perception is adjusted to the angelic realms.

YOU WILL NEED

1 Angelite, natural or tumbled

NOTE If you don't have an Angelite crystal, you can use Celestite, Danburite, Seraphinite or Selenite.

Angelite

WHAT TO DO

1. Sit comfortably on the floor with your legs crossed. Hold the Angelite in your left hand to the middle of your forehead.

2. Close your eyes and imagine you can breathe energy up and down your spine as you inhale and exhale. Practise breathing this energy up and down your spine to clear your spiritual spine and chakras.

3. Imagine an overcast day. See the clouds part, as a ray of white light comes through and bathes the top of your head. Absorb this brilliant white angelic light into your being through the top of your head. Allow this angelic light to pour in through your body, nurturing every cell, every fibre of your being with pure unconditional love.

4. With every inhalation, breathe in the blessings, healing and empowerment that are meant for you. Feel this pure energy coursing through your body as you receive your divine blessings, sit with that energy. Bask in it. Allow it to bathe your body internally and externally.

5. Now focus on your crown chakra (see page 18) and feel your divine connection. Stay with this energy for at least 5 minutes to allow this consciousness that transcends normal thought and the ordinary senses begin to take you beyond space and time into a state of deeper awareness.

6. It is now time to make full contact with your guardian angel. Feel your guardian angel drawing closer to you, standing before you, from the deepest centre of your heart chakra send out your longing for your guardian angel to help you in your healing and spiritual development. You may wish to ask for guidance or even your angel's name. Be still and wait for an answer. If necessary tell your conscious mind to step aside.

7. When you are ready bring yourself back to normal everyday waking reality.

Cosmic consciousness

Crystals contain a concentrated stable form of consciousness. For aeons, they have been absorbing and storing energy through the formation of the Earth and the cycles of nature. This stored energy is referred to as subtle-energy. Those who work holistically can access it through meditation and other spiritual techniques such as attunement or channelling.

Each crystal has its own unique properties because of its formation, colour, crystal system, hardness and mineral composition. The properties of crystals can also be enhanced through the processes of cutting, faceting, doping, irradiating and bonding.

To access the concentrated consciousness contained within crystals and use these insights to expand your awareness of subtle-energies and the spiritual realm is a lifetime's pursuit. It is often described as developing cosmic consciousness.

There is no one crystal that is more spiritual than any other, just as there is no colour that is more spiritual. Each crystal will allow you to access different levels of awareness and this brings knowledge. It is how you use this knowledge that is important. Knowledge should be used to develop understanding from which flows wisdom and ultimately cosmic consciousness and enlightenment.

Cosmic consciousness crystals

- Very clear crystals such as Danburite, Phenacite, Diamond, Clear Quartz, Herkimer Diamond, Apophyllite and Azeztulite will interact with your energy field by raising your vibration (by clearing away any cloudiness or blockages within your subtle bodies). You will be able to access knowledge of the highest subtle-energy realms – angels, archangels and ascended masters.

- Violet-coloured crystals such as Amethyst, Purple Fluorite, Sugilite and Charoite will take you into a fantasy world. This can be used to create your own reality (a wonderful way to create a healing sanctuary) but too much violet can make you feel detached from the world.

- Indigo-coloured crystals such as Iolite, Lapis, Blue Sapphire and Kyanite sedate the conscious mind and they are therefore good for developing psychic abilities.

- Pink crystals such as Rose Quartz, Morganite and Kunzite help you to develop empathy and compassion.

- Green crystals such as Emerald or Green Aventurine help you to develop inner harmony.

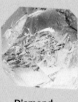

Diamond

Amethyst

Sapphire   **Kunzite**

Emerald

Attunement to cosmic consciousness

Crystal attunement develops your perception of subtle-energies. Each crystal will tend to interact with your energy field in a particular way, and it is worth taking a few days to tune into each crystal and therefore come to know each one fully. There are several ways you can attune to your crystal, so try different methods with each one, choosing a time and place where you will not be disturbed.

YOU WILL NEED
A crystal of your choice

NOTE Take the size of the crystal into account when making your choice. Pick one that you can hold comfortably for the period of your meditation, or that will rest easily on your chakras.

WHAT TO DO

1 Whichever crystal you choose, cleanse it before beginning the attunement process so the energies will be pure (see page 13 for information on how to do this).

2 Sit or lie in the position that is most comfortable position for you.

3 Begin by gently holding your chosen crystal in the palm of your hand. Study its surface, texture, colour and weight. What do you feel the colour of this crystal represents to you? Does it feel warmer or cooler than you thought it would?

4 Feel the creative power and life within it. Be present to it in spirit, by allowing your awareness to merge with the crystal energy.

5 If you meditate sitting down, try repeating the meditation with your crystal placed on top of your head on your crown chakra. If you meditate lying down, try repeating the meditation with your crystal placed on your third eye chakra (between and just above your eyes).

6 When you have completed the attunement process take sufficient time to ground yourself. Cleanse your crystal.

Developing your intuition

Developing your sixth sense, your intuition, is easy. You already use your other five senses – sight, touch, taste, hearing and smell. Each of these superficial senses gives you knowledge and understanding of your physical environment. Intuition is developing an awareness of subtle-energy that transcends the normal senses and moves your perception beyond the confines of physical time and space.

As you develop your intuition you get a balanced overview of the world by combining all your senses as well as your conscious and subconscious mind. You could therefore think of developing your intuition as integrating your body, mind and spirit or, as all three are collectively known, the psyche.

A peaceful, calm mind is needed to develop perception of subtle-energies. Most people are unaware of subtle-energy impressions because of their 'mind chatter'. Regular meditation practice and stress reduction techniques will calm and focus your mind, allowing you not only to develop your awareness of subtle-energy, but also giving you confidence in your intuitional abilities.

Therapy tips

- The size and clarity of the crystal sphere is unimportant. It is more important to choose one that feels good in your hand and holds your fixed attention. You will find scrying is made easier if you can find a sphere that seems to contain many levels or an internal 'light'.

- Scrying relies on focussing your eyes, fixing your gaze, bypassing your normal visual sensory input and allowing the 'psychic mist' to form. As this clears, subtle impressions appear. People who scry regularly habitually feel their physical eyes 'pulsing' as they begin to see the internal light within the crystal sphere activate.

- When your crystal sphere is not in use, keep it wrapped in a clean cloth to protect it from other energies. Some scryers prefer to use a white cloth, others black. The colour of cloth you prefer will depend on which colour distracts you the least when you are scrying.

Scrying

Crystal gazing or scrying using a sphere of Clear Quartz or Obsidian is an ancient way of moving beyond the confines of the rational mind to gain information that otherwise would not be available to you. It makes intensive and extensive use of your intuition and perception of subtle-energy impressions. Recognizing subtle-energy impressions is also helped by using deep blue or indigo crystals during meditation practice. Never scry when you are tired.

YOU WILL NEED
1 Clear Quartz crystal sphere
White candle

NOTE You may find you prefer to use an Obsidian or Smoky Quartz sphere for scrying, as these work better for some people.

WHAT TO DO

1 Charge the sphere with your energy by holding in your hands for a few minutes. Light a white candle, dim the lights in the room. Make yourself comfortable and quieten your mind with a few minutes of deep breathing.

2 Place the crystal sphere in front of you, on its own cloth, with the candle flame behind it. Focus on your question, be clear in your intent.

3 Allow your mind to move beyond the physical form of the sphere. You should feel a subtle-energetic link with the crystal through your physical eyes. You may also be aware of a mist forming around the crystal, or feel yourself spiralling or floating, or you may begin to feel asymmetrical or light-headed. These are all normal reactions.

4 Keep gazing at the crystal, where often an inner light will appear. Focus on any images that form and allow other guidance and inspiration to flow into you.

5 Never allow yourself to become exhausted. When you feel you have achieved as much as you can in one session, begin the closing down process. Wrap your crystal back in its cloth and blow out your candle.

6 Allow yourself plenty of time to come back to everyday reality. While it is fresh in your mind, make a written record of the experience to bring it into the physical realm and prevent it dissipating in the future. Don't be concerned if you can't fully understand the experience right away, fragmentary information is often built upon in subsequent sessions.

Protection

Crystals have always been used for personal protection against negative energy, which is any outside influence that seeks to control or manipulate your energy field by overriding your free will. If you know someone who is very controlling or obsessive, then you may be under their influence. Fuelled by jealousy, spite, anger, hatred, resentment and bitterness, the malefic thoughts they send in your direction plus their ill wishes or curses could damage your aura.

Protection crystals

- Topaz dispels enchantment and makes you invisible in times of emergency.
- Amethyst neutralizes negative energy.
- Black Tourmaline gives grounding and protection.
- Peridot drives away evil spirits.
- Petalite will render black magic impotent.
- Amber break spells and enchantment.
- Green Aventurine is shielding and reflective.
- Turquoise protects against the evil eye.
- Obsidian banishes demonic entities.
- Red Coral stops possession by evil spirits and keep away the effects of the evil eye.
- Aquamarine gives protection against the wiles of the devil.
- Actinolite is a shield that stops other people's negativity.
- Fire Agate gives spiritual fortitude.

Protection pouch

By combining these 13 crystals you will create a synergy of energies.

YOU WILL NEED

1 Topaz, natural or tumbled
1 Amethyst, natural or tumbled
1 Black Tourmaline, natural or tumbled
1 Peridot, natural or tumbled
1 Petalite, natural or tumbled
1 Amber, natural or tumbled
1 Green Aventurine, natural or tumbled
1 Turquoise, natural or tumbled
1 Obsidian, natural or tumbled
1 Red Coral, natural or tumbled
1 Aquamarine, natural or tumbled
1 Actinolite, natural or tumbled
1 Fire Agate, natural or tumbled
Small cloth pouch

WHAT TO DO

1 Cleanse all the crystals (see page 13 for information on how to do this).

2 Hold each crystal in turn and use the following dedication: 'From this moment onwards this crystal may only be used in the name of love, light and compassion and always for the universal highest good of all'.

3 Place all the crystals in the pouch. Carry the pouch on your person or wear it around your neck. Place it on your bedside table or under your pillow while you sleep.

Spiritual development

We are all born with the spiritual gifts of clairvoyance, clairaudience and clairsentience. Clairvoyance – clear seeing – is the ability to perceive subtle-energy as images, symbols or visions. Clairaudience – clear hearing – is the ability to perceive subtle-energy as sounds or words. Clairsentience – clear feeling – is the ability to perceive subtle-energies as sensations or emotions. Developing these gifts requires you to cultivate an awareness of subtle-energy.

Spiritual development crystals

- Iolite is known as the stone of prophecy, it actives and amplifies spiritual abilities.

- Blue Sapphire encourages you to reach for the stars, for high spiritual attainment.

- Lapis is a high intensity etheric stone that aids intuitional abilities.

- Selenite is a stone of communication and communion with the past and present. It aids telepathic links with others.

- Labradorite allows easy access to altered states of reality and prophetic dreams.

- Blue Moonstone aids psychic development by facilitating understanding of the hidden mysteries.

Iolite

Spiritual development meditation

Spending some time each day meditating is a sure-fire way of developing your awareness of subtle-energies. Meditation reduces stress and calms and focuses the mind, which allows your intuition and spiritual gifts to grow and develop. Deep blue and indigo coloured stones allow you to go deeper into your meditation, making you more receptive to subtle-energy information and impressions.

YOU WILL NEED

1 Iolite, natural or tumbled

NOTE: You can use another deep blue or indigo crystal of your choice if you do not have Iolite.

WHAT TO DO

1 Hold the Iolite crystal to your third eye chakra (between and just above your eyes).

2 Relax and allow your curiosity about the subtle realms to open. Be aware of any thoughts, impressions, visions or feelings that flow into your conscious mind. Try not to overanalyze them as this process moves beyond the physical realm into the dreamlike trance state of the imagination.

Meditation

Meditation has been used for aeons and throughout the world as a pathway to inner peace and tranquillity. There are many distinctive meditative traditions that have evolved through endless generations of spiritual exploration. Each tradition has generated specific theologies, ceremonies, visualizations and rituals. Despite the apparent differences, all meditation and prayer of all traditions is directed towards the same goal, the common theme being the bringing of human beings into direct experiential contact with the spiritual authenticity of their souls. Meditation practice stimulates harmonious, focused brain activity. This releases stress and improves your physical, emotional and spiritual wellbeing. Meditation also brings changes to your subtle-energy anatomy as energetic blocks that have developed throughout your life are slowly dissipated.

Therapy tips

- The wisdom of crystals is very subtle and it may be some time before you understand the lessons your crystal has to teach.

- Communication can be carried out not only with words, but also with feelings, thoughts and visions.

- Keep a written record of your meditation experiences in a journal. Essential knowledge and personal experiences can dissipate like dreams unless they are written down.

Crystal merging

Many people use crystals to enhance and deepen their meditation practice. Just holding a crystal and focusing on its magical beauty as a unique piece of nature can instantly transport you back to the very creation of the universe. This meditation technique allows you to merge with the consciousness of a crystal. Use it to gain wisdom, knowledge and healing from the crystal kingdom.

YOU WILL NEED
A crystal of your choice

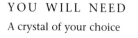

Clear Quartz

WHAT TO DO

1. Make yourself comfortable in a chair, sit on the floor or lie down on the floor, using a yoga mat or pad if you prefer.

2. If you have chosen a crystal with a termination, hold it in your left hand with the termination pointing towards your body. If you have chosen a tumbled stone or raw crystal, simply cradle it gently in your hand.

3. Allow your eyes to slowly close. Begin breathing deeply, consciously relaxing every part of your body. Begin at your feet and move slowly up your body until you reach the top of your head.

4 Do not try to control your breathing, simply be aware of the breath entering and leaving your body, the inbreath and the outbreath. Become very aware of that small space that occurs between them. What happens to you in that space? Do you go anywhere? Just observe and let go. When you are breathing gently and without strain, your body relaxed and your mind at rest, go on to the next step.

5 Gently begin to feel the crystal's subtle-energy in your left hand. Feel the energy travelling up your left arm into your shoulder and spreading across your chest and down your right arm and flowing out of the fingers of your right hand. Feel it gradually spreading through the whole of your physical body, flowing gently and easily until it slowly flows out of the top of your head and the tips of your toes.

6 At this point begin to be aware of the space around your body, as the crystal vibration flows all around you, totally enfolding you in a cloud of crystal energy. Feel yourself breathing this energy into your body as well, until there is nothing but the gently oscillating crystal vibration. Now just relax even more and simply let go, floating on your cloud of crystal energy.

7 When you are ready, allow your body to come back very slowly. Feel the weight of your body on the chair or floor. Gradually become aware of your surroundings and your normal breathing pattern. Allow yourself a little time for any feelings of light-headedness to dissipate.

Acceptance

If we ignore any aspect of ourselves we become fragmented. If we do not nurture our physical bodies they will quickly become dis-eased. If we ignore our emotional needs we invite stress into our lives. If we ignore our spirituality and fixate on worldly possessions we develop spiritual poverty.

In recent years there has been an upsurge of interest in meditation, yoga and other activities that reduce stress and aid relaxation. Through this many people have begun to open up spiritually, started to examine their life-styles and life choices, and to learn how to nurture and accept all aspects of themselves.

Crystal dreams

One of the easiest ways of accepting your spirituality is through dreams. Many crystals are defined as 'dream' crystals, and placing one of these under your pillow will help you dream meaningful dreams.

During the night while you are asleep your spiritual aspect may take over and you may find you wake up holding your dream crystal in your hand.

Many people also find their crystals move around during the night. Your subconscious may move your crystal to the area where your body needs it the most, perhaps where you have pain. The moving crystal may also be repairing damage to your aura.

YOU WILL NEED
A crystal of your choice

WHAT TO DO

1 Place the crystal under your pillow before you go to sleep. As you fall asleep, gently remind yourself that on waking you will remember any dreams that you have.

2 As soon as possible after waking, write down what you remember of your dreams. Keeping a dream journal helps you to work with your dreams and opens the gateway to spiritual understanding.

Dream crystals

- Green crystals such as Emerald, Moldavite, Aventurine, Dioptase and Verdelite help to balance the physical body and increase spiritual receptivity.

- Herkimer Diamond helps you to find solutions to problems that your conscious mind cannot access.

- Selenite and Moonstone release emotional tension.

- Sugilite, Amethyst, Charoite, Lepidolite and other violet stones open doors to other realms, remove obstacles and speed up the healing process.

Yin and Yang

The Chinese use the concepts of *yin* and *yang* to express balance within the body's energy flow. They are complementary qualities, constantly interacting. Neither can exist in isolation from the other. Their affinity to each other has a direct effect on health and harmony.

Yin is feminine, negative, passive, interior, soft, downward, inward, cold, dark and yielding. Traditionally the left side of the body is depicted as the feminine side, representing inner journeys, intuition, spiritual or psychic issues, gentleness and receiving.

Yang is masculine, positive, active, exterior, hard, upward, outward, hot, light and forceful. Traditionally the right side of the body is depicted as the masculine side, representing strength, courage, stamina and similar aggressive and dominant qualities. The right hand is the sword hand, associated with self-defence. It also represents outer journeys, money and prestige.

Yin/Yang harmony

In this crystal healing technique, balance and harmony are restored between your masculine and feminine sides, your *yin* and your *yang*. The Clear Quartz crystals facilitate healing on all levels by removing stagnant energy. The crystal termination facing inwards has an energizing effect, while the termination facing outwards has a releasing effect.

YOU WILL NEED
2 Clear Quartz, with single terminations

WHAT TO DO

1 Prepare and cleanse your crystals ready for use (see page 13 for information on how to do this).

2 Sit on the floor with your legs crossed or lie down comfortably, using a yoga mat or pad if you prefer.

Clear Quartz

3 Hold one Clear Quartz in your left hand with the termination pointing inwards. Hold the other in your right hand with the termination pointing outwards.

4 Visualize drawing energy into the crystal that is in your left hand. You may wish to visualize it as light flowing up your arm and circulating around your body.

5 As you observe the light, see it flushing away any areas of tension or pain. Allow the released energy to flow outwards from the crystal in your right hand.

6 Allow 20 minutes for your body to integrate the energies. Be ready to put down the crystals sooner if your intuition tells you that you have integrated the crystal energy more quickly.

7 Once you have integrated the energies, take sufficient time to ground yourself. Cleanse your crystals.

Index

Acknowledgements

Executive Editor Brenda Rosen
Managing Editor Clare Churly
Executive Art Editor Sally Bond
Designer James Lawrence
Photographer Janeanne Gilchrist
Picture Library Manager Jennifer Veall
Production Controller Simone Nauerth

The Publishers would like to thank Earthworks for the kind loan of some of their crystals for photography.